Christian
Adulthood

D1506572

Christian Adulthood

A JOURNEY OF SELF-DISCOVERY

Evelyn Eaton Whitehead
and James D. Whitehead

Liguori
LIGUORI, MISSOURI

Imprimi Potest: Thomas D. Picton, C.Ss.R.
Provincial, Denver Province, The Redemptorists

Published by Liguori Publications, Liguori, Missouri
www.liguori.org

Adapted from the previously published book *Seasons of Strength: New Visions of Adult Christian Maturing* by Evelyn Eaton Whitehead and James D. Whitehead, published by Doubleday & Company, 1984.

Library of Congress Cataloging-in-Publication Data

Whitehead, Evelyn Eaton.
    Christian adulthood : a journey of self-discovery / Evelyn Eaton Whitehead and James D. Whitehead.—1st ed.
        p.   cm.
    Includes bibliographical references.
    ISBN 0-7648-1284-X
    1. Adulthood. 2. Life cycle, Human—Religious aspects—Christianity. 3. Maturation (Psychology)—Religious aspects—Christianity. 4. Self-perception—Religious aspects—Christianity. 5. Christian life. 6. Virtue. I. Whitehead, James D. II. Title.

BV4597.555.W48   2005
248.8'4—dc22   2005044128

Printed in the United States of America
09 08 07 06 05   5 4 3 2 1
First edition

For Gene and Sarianna
ad multos annos

Contents

Introduction

C hristian adulthood is the focus of this book. In it we attempt to reenvision, to see anew the patterns of power, confidence, and loss that shape maturity.

A vocation refers, first and finally, to a sense that our lives are more than accidental, that we are "for something." Whether this intimation of purpose is murky or urgently clear, we find ourselves with an ambition to do something with our lives, to be somebody. In developmental psychology this sense of direction is being explored under various titles: a life project, a life theme, or the emerging personal "dream."

The Christian tradition adds to this psychological awareness the conviction that we are called by God. A human life does not happen randomly, nor does it proceed mechanistically with the genetic code as its only guide. Our lives unfold, as we sense ourselves being led, coaxed, and invited into certain paths. Today this "call," the vocation by which we experience God's ambitious presence in our own lives, is being re-imagined. The invitation to do something special with my life does not descend upon me from external authorities, appearing predominantly as a "should" or duty. It is inscribed within me, in my fragile gifts and my best insights, and it is more than my own invention. It has taken root through the influence of loved ones, the witness of communities, and the force of cherished ideals.

This vision of a vocation suggests that it is not an elitist calling. Each of us is shaped by a confluence of our gifts and wounds and hopes, which, together, focus our lives along certain paths. Such a vision challenges that misinterpretation of the scriptural phrase "Many are called but few are chosen," which understands vocation narrowly, as limited to only a few in the community of faith. The deep passivity engendered by this restrictive view of a Christian vocation left most laypersons both uncalled and unchosen, with no special religious purpose in life.

We sense today that we are called not to a static "state" in life, but to a journey. In my vocation I am invited in a certain direction, coaxed along a particular route or career (the word *career* itself means "path," or "trajectory"). Christian vocation, rooted in our best and deepest hopes for our lives, leads us along certain careers, supported by particular lifestyles, focused on the promise of the kingdom of God. Amid the random and conflicting events of our lives, individual and shared, we detect pattern and purpose. We have this sense that we are called. Hard put to "prove" or even clarify this call, we nonetheless sense the invitation as we are lured to follow certain paths.

This Christian instinct about vocation leads us to imagine God's presence in everyday life, drawing us toward certain life choices. We are led toward specific commitments of love and work. And we find our vocations confirmed in the strangest ways: in the detours of a career; in the fruitfulness of celibacy; in the gift of a child with a disability.

This ancient conviction that God is about something special in our lives is finding new and exciting expression today. Here we revisit ancient and contemporary images of the maturing of a Christian life. The goal is to re-imagine the movement of God in our lives as we explore a contemporary theology of Christian vocation.

Chapter one offers a new image for Christian maturity, suggesting that a vocation is to be "played" rather than worked. In chapter two vocation is discussed as the personal "dream," which can be fostered or frustrated by other ambitions active in the community. Chapter three and chapter four trace the journey of a maturing Christian from child of God through the discipleship of young adulthood and into the stewardship of mature middle years. In chapter five we recognize that maturing takes time: many seasons are required for that seasoning of instincts which marks us as Christian adults. In chapter six we discuss the new faces of Christian virtue in contemporary life, particularly the virtue of self-intimacy as the growing ability to accept and to love the person I am being called to be. In chapter seven we conclude by confronting issues of special significance for Christian maturity today: our propensity to grow in power and accept weakness. To mature is to become more powerful, but it is also to become more tolerant of our own enduring and even startling weaknesses. Maturity thus demands an increasing familiarity with personal power—its shape, its source, its goal.

If the focus of this book is adult maturing, its central dynamic is the imagination. To change is to re-imagine. Vocations fail when we cannot imagine that our lives have any special purpose or worth. Growth happens as we are able to foresee the next stage of the journey. Healing has a chance only if we can picture the possibility of forgiveness. The renaissance in Christian life today springs from the imagination: laypersons recognizing, with surprise, their own religious callings; women imagining a new potency; church leaders picturing a more mutual way of ministering in a community. While we do not here formally discuss the imagination, we recognize that it is evident throughout.

Adult maturing and the imagination enjoy a special intimacy: it is in our images that we harbor our hopes and expectations about life. Some of these images are holy and invite us to growth; others are the twisted and compulsive demands that frustrate our development. But all live in the imagination. From this volcanic storehouse arise our terrifying nightmares, our inspired visions, our fantasies of failure and death. The imagination seems at once ally and enemy. It encourages our best efforts while, simultaneously, it casts shadows that remind us of frightening possibilities that may await. In our maturing we are invited to approach this ambiguous power within. In this book we explore this "approach" in the metaphors of taming, befriending, seasoning.

Central among the images of this volume are the play of a vocation and the seasoning of senses. Mature play includes an ability to "test the leeway" (Erik Erikson). This is a goal and promise of Christian adulthood: the mature strength to "test the leeway" in the traditional roles of Christian life so that we might hand these on, fresh and faithful, to the future. And the process by which such maturity is attained is the seasoning of senses, the gradual transformation of our instincts—of power and sexuality and justice—by the life and witness of Jesus Christ.

Finally, a word on how we hope this book will be used. We bring together here the social sciences and Christian theology in a dialogue on themes of adult maturing. To these two conversation partners we invite a third—the reader. This volume is meant as a practical reflection on the maturing of the adult Christian. The life experience of the reader makes a critical contribution. We invite readers to confirm and to challenge the discussions here in the light of their adult journey. To help this process we have added reflective exercises at the conclusion of each chapter. Readers of our earlier books repeatedly tell us how useful they find these reflective opportunities. We hope that you will as well.

Christian
Adulthood

CHAPTER ONE

The Leap
of a Vocation

A quiet revolution is occurring in the land. Ancient distinctions between clergy and laity are giving way. A time-honored separation between Christians who "have vocations" and those who do not is being bridged. This is a revolution of the imagination: new visions of Christian life—of adult faith, of ministry, of community—are being born. At the core of this profound change stands a re-imagining of a Christian vocation.

Every Christian is called. And we are called over a lifetime. The first conviction entails a non-elitist vision of a vocation. A Christian vocation is not a "specialty"; it refers not only to the priesthood or vowed religious life, but to the particular direction and purpose that every maturing believer is expected to find and to follow. On Vocation Sunday, then, we pray for all of us. It is when the sacrament of baptism takes root that a vocation is begun, as the believer embarks on a life journey toward and with God. This non-elitist vision of Christian vocations arises from a more vigorous sense of adult faith and

1

will, in time, give new shape to the structures of Christian ministry.

If we are each called, in different and particular ways, we are also called again and again. A vocation takes a lifetime. This insight gives vocation a more developmental sense. Our vocation grows and changes as we come into a fuller realization of our adult journey of faith.

A vocation is not a once-and-for-all call in young adulthood (to follow this career or enter this religious congregation). It is a lifelong conversation with God. Like any rich conversation, it is patterned by periods of spirited exchange, times of strain and argument, and intervals of silence. In such a developmental vision of a vocation, fidelity is more than memory. To be faithful entails more than recalling an early invitation; it requires that we remain in the conversation. Our fidelity must be mobile because the conversation continues.

A Christian vocation is a gradual revelation—of me to myself by God. Over a lifetime I gradually learn the shape of my life. And it takes a lifetime. At twenty-one, few of us could bear to learn all the turns and detours of the upcoming journey. Thus God reveals us gradually to ourselves. In this vision, a vocation is not some external role visited upon us. It is our own religious identity; it is who we are, trying to happen.

If a vocation is a lifelong invitation, we can see that it is an extraordinary exercise of the imagination. First, I envision my life moving in a particular direction. From scattered hints and uncertain inclinations I begin to envision the shape of my life. I am, most often, brought to see this direction; this vision comes as a gift and sometimes as a command.

But I not only envision the purpose of my life, I must create it as well. This is the second stroke in imagining a vocation. My life unfolds, demanding choices of love and work. It is in the face of these choices that I both receive my vocation and invent it. A vocation is not only vision; it includes my decision to live out this vision in the choices that give my life its actual shape.

An adult identity, like a Christian vocation, is an imaginative creation. I come to see—if I am fortunate—that the details of my life are more than haphazard or random. I may catch a glimpse of a design in the very particularity of my life—these parents, these abilities, in this place at this time. There is a plot here! This recognition of a plot—a sequence in my life, a connection between my past and my future—becomes the core of an adult identity. This is who I am and what I am for. To come to this conviction is an exercise of the imagination; it is also the beginning of a vocation.

At the outset of adult life the challenge, both psychologically and religiously, is to imagine what my life is to be about. In our senior years we are invited to affirm, in retrospect, the shape and goodness of this most peculiar plot. And during our middle years we can be required—by experiences of profound change or loss or stagnation—to re-imagine the pattern and purpose of life. Sometimes reversals or disappointments tempt us to despair: there is no sense to it all. Hope eludes us, leaving us mired in this experience of "nonsense." Unable to picture a plot or purpose here, we may lose our way—both identity and vocation seem gone. It is imagination with its new visions of hope that can rescue us from this impasse. Thus we can come to see that vocations fail, not when earlier visions undergo change, but when we can no longer imagine that God is about something in our lives.

The Creation of a Vocation

In the Church today we are involved in reunderstanding many of the images in which our faith has been expressed. The central image of creation is itself under review, as we recognize the many ways in which Christians have attempted to acknowledge our radical dependence before God. There are intriguing connections between images of creation and of vocation. We will consider three images of creation here to see what they say to us about the reality of Christian vocation.

One way in which Christians have understood creation is as something that we inhabit. Here we imagine creation as God's production, but a production now fully accomplished. Ours is a world fully formed, fully imagined by God. In such a stable environment we see our lives guided by "natural laws," rules built in at the beginning. In such a vision, a vocation is likely to be seen as a clear role, stable and unchanging. As adults, we each inhabit a proper "state in life," whether clergy or lay, married or vowed religious. Each is called to enter one of these vocational "states" and live faithful to its rules and guidelines. The role of imagination in such a vision is likely to be restricted to recognizing the state in life to which we are called. There is little enthusiasm for inventing new roles or improvising on those already given. Such inventiveness on our part would seem to suggest that God had been somehow negligent or mistaken "in the beginning."

A second vision that influences our understanding of vocations sees creation as something that is worked. Whether finished or still in process, creation here is imagined in the industrial metaphor of work. God created the world in a six-day (work) week. After the Sabbath rest, the enterprise was turned over to us. We creatures take up this work of creation "in the sweat of our brow." The chief feature of this image is its seriousness. We may participate in God's creation, but we do so earnestly and soberly. Purposefulness is a central value in such a model, leaving little room for experimentation or delight.

A third way to imagine creation is as something that is being played. This image of creation, which emphasizes inventiveness and delight, is an ancient one. Plato turned to this metaphor in his description of human nature: "Humans…have been constructed as a plaything of god and this is, in fact, the finest thing about them" (Laws 7.803c). Shakespeare wrote that "all the world's a stage" on which humans play out their

4

lives. Both these writers understood the play of creation as our performance of roles already fully scripted by a divine author. Play is thus essentially imitative: we find our joy in replaying divinely cast roles already given.

Theologians have been exploring another interpretation of play, one that may allow us to re-imagine more vigorously both creation and vocation. John Dominic Crossan and others suggest that a Christian theology of creation take more notice of play in its most creative aspect. In play (and so, in the play of a vocation) we do not simply repeat an already scripted role; we also invent and improvise. When we play we do not just imitate, we also create. Applying the image of play to creation itself, we can imagine creation as open-ended and in that sense unfinished. It is a creation still being played. We are participants in this creation, both replaying the classic roles and scripting new scenes in this continuing story. Scenes from the past give Christians guidelines for a plot that bears repeating. But it is an unfinished drama that demands our creative participation not only in response but in initiative and choice as well.

The image of creation as play is attractive in its creativity and delight, but it carries with it several inherent prejudices. Western culture bears three crucial biases about play: play has often been seen as childish, frivolous, and unreal. Childhood is judged to be the proper domain of play. Lacking full rationality and responsibility, children can only play at life. Once matured, adults should set aside play in favor of the duties and demands of their lifework. Artists and, in our culture, athletes may continue their preoccupation with "child's play," but they serve the rest of us not as models but as refuges from the serious business of adult life.

A second bias against play is that it is frivolous; we depart from weighty, adult matters by "playing around." In the book of Exodus there is a passage that uses play in this pejorative sense. Describing the idolatry and immorality of the people during Moses' absence, the account notes that "the people sat down to eat and drink, and rose up to revel" (Exodus 32:6). The suggestion here is that play is not just some harmless distraction but an excess that turns the people away from Yahweh. For serious Christians, too, play has often been interpreted pejoratively. It is always a trivial pursuit, sometimes even sinful.

In a third bias, play is understood not only as childish and frivolous but as unreal. The Latin word for play, ludere, survives in our own word *illusion*. To play is to pretend, to occupy a fictitious role. To play is to step out of reality, to impersonate and even deceive.

With these cultural biases alive among us, we may wonder if play can be rescued as an image of creation and vocation. To undertake such a re-imagining of play we need authorization. Are there in Scripture any hints that may help us envision play in its more positive and creative meanings? A clue may be found in the Book of Proverbs. Here we encounter Wisdom, the feminine form of God, describing her role in creation:

> ...I was beside him, like a master worker;
> and I was daily his delight,
>   rejoicing before him always,
>   rejoicing in his inhabited world
>   and delighting in the human race

PROVERBS 8:30–31

Innumerable questions, linguistic and theological, surround this strikingly non-Israelitic picture of creation. Who is Wisdom, this companion and player with the Creator? Hebrew texts differ, some translating the first description as "master crafter," some as "child." The choice of child settles a number of issues: the Creator's companion would be a playful child, not an adult partner who might be construed as a consort. But apart from the suggestion of a feminine partner in the process, this story suggests connections among creation, play, and delight. Creation here is neither the serious work of an industrious maker nor the solitary invention of a bachelor god. It is rather with companionship and delight that creation is played.

Vocation As a Leap

If we can imagine creation as still being played—with us as players and partners with God and with the final act not written—then we are better able to envision the play of a vocation. This re-imagining will demand that we toughen and expand our notion of play, rescuing it from both pious sentiment and cultural bias. A useful guide here is psychologist Erik Erikson, in his book *Toys and Reasons.*

Erikson takes up Plato's suggestion that play originates in the random leaps of the child. He then points to three distinct elements of these gratuitous and energetic hounds. First, the child leaps out of delight. For no special purpose ("except," the harassed parent may counter, "to drive me crazy!") the child leaps and jumps repeatedly. Performed simply for the delight of it, the leap is for its own sake.

Second, such a leap is a move against gravity. The child, in Erikson's phrase, "tests the leeway," challenging the gravity and givenness of life. If play is part delight, it is also assertion and contest.

Third, to leap is to fall. To launch oneself upward is to undertake an effort that will inevitably bring one back to earth. Fallings and failings seem essential aspects of the leaping that is play. Delight, testing the limits, falling—these ingredients of human play are also elements of a maturing vocation.

A vocation is a leap: we often speak of such a significant life choice as a leap of faith; sometimes it can feel like a leap in the dark! In a moment of life commitment, I "go beyond" the information available and give myself to something that escapes my sure control. How can I be sure that I should marry this

person or join this religious congregation or pursue this career? Committing ourselves in these ways, we are likely to sense
the risk—even the foolhardiness—of such a venture. And yet
we want to make the leap. As young adults, we sense that we
need to leave the familiar confines of our families and our own
adolescent selves and set out for parts unknown and untested.
Idealism and romance help propel us into the commitments
that mark our twenties. And, like the child, we need to leap—
to risk—again and again if we are to keep our vocations lively.
In a developmental understanding, we see a vocation not as a
one-time leap that lands us safely in the middle of a stable
vocational "state," but as an ongoing exercise of commitment
that requires agility and grace.

A Leap of Delight

We may imagine a vocation as a leap, but how is it a leap of
delight? One's vocation is a path to be followed in pursuit of
the Lord. Most of us might agree that a vocation lived faithful-
ly should be satisfying, but "delight" still feels foreign. This
aspect of play seems difficult to incorporate into an image of a
Christian calling. If we have grown up in the belief that holiness comes in sober obedience to the "shoulds" and "oughts"
in life, there may be little room to see our vocations as delight-
ful. The delight of a vocation is rooted in a sense of its goodness and "fit." I delight in the shape that my own life takes as
I experience the way it fits my own particular gifts and limits.
It is not just the "right" thing for me to do with my life, it is
good for me as well.

How is a Christian vocation "for its own sake"? This ele-
ment of play is not easily celebrated in a religious tradition
steeped in a profound purposefulness. In marriage we make
love in order to have children; our religious and priests live as
celibates so that they can serve better; we strive to live virtuous
lives in order to merit heaven. With these good purposes so

much a part of our sense of adult commitment, how can we experience our vocations "for their own sakes"? It may help here to recall the experience of liturgy, so central in Christian communal life. Liturgy, as our celebration of the Lord's enlivening and healing presence, is for its own sake. Romano Guardino has observed that liturgy is "pointless, but full of significance." Celebration arises among us in counterbalance to work and achievement. It is not, finally, for something else; it is for its own sake. But if our religious awareness of creation is couched exclusively in images of work and achievement, it will be difficult to envision the ongoing creation of our own lives as entailing celebration or delight.

Finally, the awareness of a vocation as a leap of delight must be more than theoretical. I must be able to savor my own vocation, to delight in the design that emerges as my life moves with God. In each vocation, whatever its shape, there is challenge and pain and stress. But a vocation holds more than this; we know the reward of accomplishment, the joy of presence, the comfort of peace as well. My appreciation of my own vocation deepens as I am able to name its delights for me. It is here that I celebrate "for its own sake" the shape that my life has taken.

Testing the Leeway

If a Christian vocation begins in a leap of faith and matures through a series of graceful bounds, it also "tests the leeway." This aspect of play reminds us of the limited mobility of our lives. The child's leap is purposeless, but it does have an inner economy: to see how high she can go. Gravity restricts how far she can jump, but it doesn't keep her from leaping. Erikson finds in this aspect of play a model of human maturity. We always find ourselves in a context of limited mobility. The limits of our own abilities, the constraints of the environment and the historical setting—these restrict us. It is within, sometimes even against, the boundaries of these givens that we leap. It is in the interplay of possibility and limit that our vocations take shape. With no sense of limit, our lives lack definition and responsibility; with no feel of mobility, they grow stagnant and unplayful.

That a Christian vocation is an arena for such maturing interplay seems especially clear. The lifestyle I choose—married person, single adult, vowed religious, priest—has been chosen before many times in Christian experiences. As I live out this role I experience both its limits and its flexibility. I am not a priest or a married person "in general"; I am this priest, this spouse, this particular adult—my own version of this traditional role. Our vocation matures in this testing of the limits as we experience the tension between the limits that define our chosen roles and the flexibility that our own gifts and insights bring to them.

The Church today is alive with this testing of leeway in our vocations. As a people, we are exploring whether the role of community leader will flex enough to allow married people to serve in this way; gay and lesbian adults are pursuing lives that are both genuinely Christian and fully sexual; women are discerning new ways of leadership in the Church. If these are examples of serious struggle, they are also instances of creative play. In the assertive interplay of these encounters the Church's vocation is itself being tested and matured. In our resolution of these contests, we are writing the next chapter in the Church's history; we are playing out an as yet unimagined future.

We are reminded here how robust play is. It is more than frivolity or mere diversion; its fruits are more than simple delight. A Christian vocation demands that we be energetic and assertive players, willing to contest, able to push against the limited mobility of our religious heritage. Without this interplay, without the jostling and contesting involved, the tradition will stagnate. In the interplay of our vocations, we enliven both our own lives and the life of the Church. We play out in our own lives the sacred story of Jacob wrestling with Yahweh, as together they grappled toward a new, more mature relationship.

Falling and Failure

The vigor of this contest brings us to the third aspect of play: falling. Here again we learn that play is not without its lessons; we are reminded that in leaping we must be prepared to fall. In the rough-and-tumble of play the child learns that to fall is neither disastrous nor disgraceful. In fact, it is an integral part of the leap. The challenge for both the child and the maturing adult is to allow room for the fall. How do we learn to fall gracefully in our vocations?

This question brings us to a theology of failure. As Christians, with our special sensitivity to "the Fall," we have been reluctant to imagine failure as having a place—perhaps even a necessary role—in the maturing of vocation. If creation is a "finished product," there is little room for mistakes. Failure is easily identified with infidelity and falling with sin. In Christian spirituality the ideal of perfection has made its special contribution to the crippling of play. To play is to chance falling; if falling is always moral failing, there seems little justification for Christian play. And many Christians have come to such a sense in their vocations. Finding themselves in roles that are stable but inflexible, they are unable to play because there is no place to fall.

There are, however, some clues in our religious tradition concerning a theology of failure. In our Easter liturgy we recall the original fall as a *felix culpa*, a happy fault. How can a failure of such tragic proportion be construed as "happy"? Its happiness is, of course, that it brought Jesus Christ into our midst. Through the fall, God has become tangible to us. Ironically the fall itself has become graceful. Tragic though it was, the fall was also profoundly fruitful. In retrospect it even appears integral to God's loving design.

We can come to sense the place of fall in the play of our own lives as well. As our vocations mature, we experience the fruitfulness of failings. Every adult life is generously scarred with failure. In our love, in our work, things have not gone as we had hoped. Sometimes we were at fault; sometimes others seem to have been to blame; sometimes it "just happened." Early on we tend to respond to such failure with anger, regret, shame. In midlife we may come to see these events in a new perspective. In the graceful light of retrospection, we realize that these happenings were not just hurtful. Our wounds have contributed in strange but tangible ways to the substance of our vocations. A failure at an aborted early career helped turn me to my present work. Or the loss of an important early love I see now as a necessary, if painful, part of my maturing in intimacy. Such midlife reconciliations invite us to embrace and welcome these falls as genuine parts of who we are. We are able to celebrate the shape of our vocations, knowing both the strangeness and the goodness of our lives with God.

A maturing vocation likely brings another experience of failure. This is what we might call a developmental "fall from innocence." The first leaps of a youthful vocation, energized by idealism and romantic vision, often include high expectations of a Church without flaw and a religious tradition without ambiguity. As we mature in the Church, we may be felled by the failings and shortcomings—even the sinfulness—we find there. This disillusionment functions as a developmental parallel to the painful but necessary realization in adolescence that "my parents are not perfect." The illusions that were necessary and useful to our biological and ecclesial childhood must fail us if we are to mature. How else will we know to put them aside? When we can acknowledge the necessary failure of these illusions, without resorting simply to bitterness and blame, we gain a more mature tolerance for ambiguity and error. The ideological vigor of young adulthood is softened as we play through the failures that are part of a maturing vocation.

At this point we can begin to re-imagine what it means to be a graceful player. Mature play does not include rising above all mistakes; it does entail learning to fall gracefully. The acrobat or the gymnast might serve as a model of one who has learned to fall well. When she comes down "wrong"—turning an ankle or landing on her head—the acrobat learns to bounce up with a flourish as though the fall were part of the act. And, in the larger sense of play, it is.

But every metaphor limps. Sometimes it is best not to leap up and go on as if nothing has happened; some falls demand immediate attention and take time to heal. These falls remind us of the importance of the environment to our vocational play. If we leap, we need a safe place to land.

A Place to Play

Our discussion so far may give the impression that Christians play their vocations privately or in solitude. The maturing of a vocation is influenced by the places where we play. Community is the context of vocational play; it is the Christian community that is our privileged playground.

British psychiatrist D. W. Winnicott has studied the first environment of human play, the relationship of child and parent. It is in this earliest interplay that the child develops a sense of self distinct from the parent. The child learns here the earliest lessons of intimacy by playing before and against this nurturing person who is "other" but trustworthy. Such a parent allows the child to leap, giving boundaries and rules that can be tested, and supporting the child when she falls. One of Winnicott's special contributions to a theory of play is his observation of the connection between trust and concentration. Only in a trusting environment will the child be able to give full attention to play. Without this concentration the child is too distracted to play well. With it she learns "to be alone in the presence of another." This ability is the foundation both of the mature play of Christian prayer and of the lifelong interplay of friendship and marriage.

Winnicott's brief observations help us appreciate the role of a Christian community as a trusting and trustworthy environment. Such a community—whether parish or family or religious congregation—provides the place to play out a vocation. It encourages leaping; it gives boundaries, rules, resistance against which individuals can test their own life choices; it offers a place to land.

We speak more colloquially of needing "a place to crash." We mean somewhere to come down after our daily leaps, a place that provides solid footing or cushioning arms for our descent. An unsupportive community resists this. It interprets leaping as restlessness and instability. It sees testing the leeway as ingratitude or infidelity. It responds to our falls with embarrassment or blame. In this kind of community, our leaping comes to a halt or we go next door to play. Such a community stagnates in seriousness and self-defense. The trusting community has managed to learn the meaning of play, probably by recognizing its own leaps and stumbles. A flexible and safe place to play, a community of this kind fulfills its function as a sacrament. It is a sign of the continuing play of God's creation, a witness that Wisdom continues to "play everywhere in the world, delighting to be with the children of humanity."

Finally, it is in a trusting community that we learn the profound connections among play and trust and intimacy. In *Adaptation to Life*, George E. Vaillant summarizes this interplay:

> It is hard to separate capacity to trust from capacity to play, for play is dangerous until we can trust both ourselves and our opponents to harness rage. In play, we must trust enough and love enough to risk losing without despair, to bear winning without guilt, and to laugh at error without mockery.

As we tame failing and falling, we become mature players in our vocations. Better able to risk and test and fall, we show the next generation of believers the style of Christian play. We witness that a vocation is a lively, fragile, flexible gift to be played with energy. And in the interplay we predict the shape of Christian community for the future.

Reflective Exercise

You are encouraged to take a few moments in a quiet place, away from distractions, to reflect on the special movements of your own life. After some moments of quieting yourself, let the following questions arise within you:

1. With what kind of leap did my own vocation, my own adult Christian life, begin?
2. Where do I continue to delight in my life, as good for its own sake?
3. Where am I testing the leeway in my adulthood? How do I experience the tension between the "roles" in my life and my own unique way of living them out?
4. What "falls" have been an important part of my maturing? Are there failures or mistakes in my past that I can recognize, in retrospect, as "happy faults"?

CHAPTER TWO

Christian Maturing: The Story of Three Dreams

A Christian vocation is not an elitist calling but an invitation to make something good and holy of our lives. The path may lead me to marry or remain single; it may lead me into the business world or a service profession or the priesthood. Whether loudly or barely heard, it is always a call that draws us to use our abilities to follow Christ's witness of challenge and care for the world.

In this lifelong conversation with God, we continue to hear hints and rumors of who we might become, of what we are to do. Only gradually over many decades do we come to glimpse what God imagines our life might become. Testing our insights and hopes against our abilities and environment, we very gradually come into our vocations. A vocation is thus not a mystical or abstract notion; it is the changing shape of our adult lives as Christians.

This maturing of our hopes and commitments expectably

takes a lifetime. In our forties we learn things about our strengths and weaknesses that we could not have known in our twenties; in our seventies we are still being revealed to ourselves. It takes a lifetime for God to show us who we are. Fidelity to a vocation, as we noted in chapter one, is not just an act of memory. It is the decision to remain in the conversation. Continuing to communicate with God, to listen for God's voice in the successes and failures, delights and disasters, of an adult life, we are more surely revealed to ourselves.

Our vocations mature through the revelations and purifications of such a lifelong conversation.

This developmental vision of a Christian vocation brings it into dialogue with Daniel J. Levinson's notion of the "dream." In *Seasons of a Man's Life*, Levinson explores adult growth as a development of a dream or life ambition. Here, a dream is not a nocturnal fantasy but a life project—an enduring and growing sense of what I am to do in life. This dream is what I most want to do with my life. Such a life ambition runs below every specific plan and job; it struggles to survive every change and detour in adult life.

A Vocation As a Dream

A dream, and a vocation, is what I want to do "when I grow up." The five-year-old who wants to be a truck driver or a nurse or an astronaut gives an early hint of the dream. In our late teens and early twenties the dream emerges, often with much vigor. Readying us to enter the adult world, our imagination fills with ambitious plans or tentative hopes. Levinson's research recalls a special feature of the early dream: its idealism. The young woman wants to become not simply a doctor but a pioneering neurosurgeon; the young man wants to become not merely a writer but an award-winning novelist. The devout young Christian's ambition may be not only helping others but traveling as a missionary to poverty-stricken peoples in far-off lands. Psychologically, we need the energy of such idealism to propel us into the complex and confusing world of adulthood. The coming decades will see a mellowing of this idealism as our dream comes to fit us better.

During our twenties the dream undergoes much testing and renegotiation. On the inside we ask, "Am I up to such a vision?" Do I have the stuff to live out this vocation? And on the outside we are testing: Will the world allow me to do this? Is there room in the Church for such a dream? With enthusiasm or tentativeness we try out our dreams, test our vocations in the real world. Sometimes this testing demands that we clarify a dream that is powerful but vague. The young woman wants to serve others, to help humanity—but how? What specific path is this desire to follow? Another young person finds himself with a powerful and very clear dream: to be a teacher. But experience, in school and elsewhere, begins to indicate that the dream will not be realized in this specific form. He is challenged to reinterpret his dream. How can his goals find expression in another career? What ambition lies under this specific vision of service and care? For many young adults the decade of the twenties is spent testing out these early dreams.

But something else may happen during this critical time: the dream may be lost. My dream, my vocation abides in my imagination. Without nurturance it can wither and disappear. Either from lack of support or because we ourselves cannot believe in them, our dreams may be set aside. Confused or frightened, I may abandon the dream. One way out, which makes our abandoning the dream easier, is to find someone else who seems to have a strong sense of purpose—a spouse or leader or religious congregation—and join my life to that dream. Or I may settle for living out the dream that a parent or teacher has for me. It may be decades later that I come to realize what I have done. At this point I am invited to an important and probably painful reconciliation with my own lost dream.

Before examining these reconciliations in midlife, we will consider some connections between the psychological notion of a life's dream and Christian convictions concerning vocation. First, each is understood as an expression of my deepest and best hopes for my life. They also share a common habitat: the imagination. It is in images that we envision our dream and our vocation. Whether these are "just fantasies" or realizable hopes will take time to determine. But we have vocations and life dreams only if we are attentive to the imagination. For Christians, both dreams and vocations are vehicles of revelation. The Old Testament is filled with stories of dreams and visions in which our ancestors recognized God's will for them. In the visions and hopes that make up our vocations we, like they, learn who we are to be; we are revealed to ourselves. Finally, a vocation differs from a dream in a special way: a vocation is a dream personalized. A dream is often explained in terms of factors of environment or heredity. As Christians we believe that a vocation involves more; it is God's dream for us. Rooted in more than chance or fate, our vocation is what God has in mind—or better, in imagination—for us. In my vocation I am being imagined by God; God's dream for my life comes gradually to light.

Reconciliations With the Dream

In our twenties we explore and test the dream, making those choices that launch it toward realization or decline. I choose a career; I marry this person; I enter religious life. These commitments set us in pursuit of certain life ambitions. Usually in our thirties we are preoccupied with the work that our dreams demand: raising our children, working at our ministry, building up an adult sense of competence and stability. Over these first decades of adult experience, we are fully involved in "making something of ourselves"—we are living out the dream, following a vocation. We are accumulating the information and insight into ourselves that may eventually lead us to reassess our dream.

In midlife many of us find ourselves reexamining our dreams. A vocation, a dream, is an ongoing revelation; it is to be expected along the way that we feel the need to revisit and reevaluate the direction our lives are taking. This "return" of the dream, which demands special attention in midlife, is part of the maturing of a vocation. It plays an important role in what our colleague J. Gordon Myers calls "the purification of expectations."

This reconciliation with the dream in midlife can take different shapes. In a first pattern we may be invited to come to terms with the way our dream has gone. Here the challenge is one of fit: to appreciate the ways in which my earlier dream, idealistic and grand, has found its more realistic shape in my life. I have not become all I hoped for; I may not have achieved the extraordinary visions of youth. But I have become this particular, if peculiar, version of the dream. In a mood of mellowness I am invited to embrace my life and this vocation, rather than an earlier, perhaps more grandiose version. The invitation in this reconciliation is, in Levinson's terms, one of "de-illusionment." Not disillusionment, but de-illusionment: we are called to let go of some of the necessary illusions of youth. By now these illusions—about my talent or resourcefulness or influence—should be less necessary. As I become more comfortable with the shape of my own life, I can let go of self-descriptions that are more ideal than real. More self-accepting, I can rejoice in who I am becoming, even while mourning parts of the dream that will not be realized. This reconciliation is one face of a midlife purification of expectations.

A second kind of reconciliation may be demanded as I recognize the tyranny of the dream in my life. In our twenties we may give ourselves to a life ambition—with a vengeance. We are ready to sacrifice everything else to reach our goal, whether it is success or fame or even holiness. And we may even achieve it. But by midlife a dream so compulsively pursued is likely to have become a tyranny. Under its sway we have sacrificed too much—friends, family, health, peace of mind. We pray now to be delivered from the curse of our success. Reconciliation with my dream demands rescue from its tyranny. I am invited to recover parts of my life that I have ignored or denied in the all-out pursuit of narrow goals. I am reminded that a dream is but part of me; when it becomes a tyrant, it destroys other aspects of my life. In this reexamination I am called to forgive myself. Self-blame and guilt may be strong as I realize what I have done to myself. Forgiveness is part of the reconciliation demanded now.

In a third reconciliation we may be called to recover a dream deferred. This challenge occurs when I recognize that I have lost an earlier dream. I may have set it aside as I took a temporary job to meet the financial needs of my family; twenty years later the temporary job continues. Or I may have been talked out of my dream by a parent or someone else who judged it to be foolish or impractical. Now at forty-five or fifty, I sense this forgotten dream arise anew, asking again to be heard. Here, too, forgiveness is central to the reconciliation. As the dream returns I am tempted to blame myself or, more likely, "those others" who kept me from my dream. To recover this lost dream I will need to forgive this part of my past. If I cannot forgive, much of the new energy of the returning dream will dissipate in anger or regret.

In midlife the lost dream returns to a life that is intricately connected with the lives of other people—family, colleagues, companions. No longer the unencumbered youth to whom the dream first announced itself, we are bound with the commitments of the past several decades. Is there room for a new dream in such a life? Do the responsibilities of my previous choices crowd out any possibility of new choices, new directions for my life? In this reconciliation I am asked to introduce the returning dream into the network of my existing commitments. In the vigorous dialogue that is likely to ensue, I try to reenvision and revise my vocation.

Another kind of reconciliation, not reported in Levinson's research, is witnessed in Christian communities today. This is the end of one dream and the beginning of another. An earlier dream has been achieved; narrow or not, it has been lived out. Now in midlife, new ambitions, perhaps not even imaginable in an earlier Church, are being born within me. New revelations are being heard; a new stage of the journey with God would begin if I could let myself hear the new voice of God and, with fidelity, follow it. This more radical breaking in of a new dream reminds us of the importance of our social context. Dreams do not arise in isolation; Christians do not receive vocations in private. As the Church and our communities change and mature, new dreams are set loose.

A Community's Dream

Personal vocations are imbedded in social contexts. Our dreams begin within our families. They are nurtured or frustrated in neighborhoods, parishes, and schools—those settings where we learn what to expect from life. These places are themselves more than just a collection of individual dreams. A social setting, especially a family or a parish, can have a dream of its own. A group's special purpose, its shared ambitions and goals can be recognized as its corporate vocation.

The family is the original arena of our dreams. Parents are busy not only with the pursuit of their own life ambitions but with fostering their children's dreams. An inner discipline that as parents we must learn to practice is to distinguish our own hopes from the fragile, beginning dreams of our children. Parents come, sometimes slowly and painfully, to know the hard truth of Christian stewardship: in our children we are the

nurturers of dreams, the guardians of vocations that we neither control nor fully understand.

But a family is more than a collection of individual vocations. A family gradually develops its own collective dream:
this group of people, responding to the many invitations of
God that have both brought them together and put them in
tension with each other, slowly forges its own set of values and
hopes. The lifestyle and decisions that give this family its uniqueness also define its dream of Christian life. Such a family dream
is often fragile. The busyness of everyday life can distract us
from one another; we often seem to lack the time to share our
deepest hopes. And so our sense of common aspiration can be
lost or at least rarely celebrated. Or a family dream can be
warped, with the ambition or needs of one member serving as
constraint on all the others. But a family in which a Christian
dream is alive fulfills the rhetoric of our faith: the family becomes a "domestic church."

Just as a Christian family matures in the development of
its dream, so too a Christian community grows as it becomes
aware of its own vocation. A parish, for example, expectably
builds a shared sense of Christian purpose. How does such a
corporate vocation arise? In its public actions a community hands
on some version of the Christian dream, whether as an exciting
hope or as a withered memory. In every liturgical celebration
and educational effort a faith community announces its dream.

The religious development of the members of the community depends on this shared dream. Until recently, "religious
formation" usually has referred to the initial training of vowed
religious or priests. Yet formation of its members in faith is
what any faith community must be about. And the vitality of
the community's dream is crucial in this religious formation of
all its members.

In religious formation, a faith community invites its members to join their dreams to the corporate vision of the group.
The assumption here is that both the community and the indi-

vidual have a dream. The balance between the individual and the corporate dream is most important. A faith community is not a neutral zone in which individuals pursue their separate vocations. Nor does a community provide vocations for individuals who would otherwise be directionless. Recognizing that the Spirit is alive in all believers, exciting them to life ambitions that contribute to the kingdom of God, a community of faith invites its members to pursue their vocations as part of the community's larger dream and purpose. Further, a community offers models of many specific ways to follow a Christian vocation. It displays—in its liturgies and program for social justice, in the lives of its talented and concerned members—the Christian dream at work. The individual is invited to let his dream, her vocation, grow within and contribute to this community's hopes.

The community's corporate vocation is also challenged and changed by individual dreams. Every human vocation—and this includes each individual and community in the Church—remains in need of purification. The purification of a community's dream may begin as new dreams arise among individuals in the group. Members of a parish staff imagine new forms of collaborative ministry; board members of a Catholic hospital begin to envision more effective ways of serving the very poor; women accept new roles of leadership in their families and in their Church. Such dreams are often threatening because they challenge the adequacy and stability of the group's current vision. Since it is likely to disturb our accustomed ways of experiencing our faith, we may judge a new dream to be a mere illusion, a passing enthusiasm that will soon disappear. Yet we know from our history as a religious people that new dreams have been part of the important movements of growth and renewal among us. New dreams can break open collective hopes that have become too rigid; they can challenge ambitions that have grown too safe and shortsighted. Our religious heritage has been profoundly affected by individual dreams breaking into and altering our collective sense of purpose. We think of Francis of Assisi, Catherine of Siena, Ignatius of Loyola. But this same dynamic also happens in more ordinary ways in our faith communities today. If it is confusing, it is also to be expected. The collective dream of a community must support and challenge the growth of individual vocations, just as these individual dreams contribute to and, at times, challenge the community's dream. And both dreams, individual and corporate, must remain open to the enlivening critique and purification provided by God's continuing revelation of us to ourselves.

A community's dream also shares the vicissitudes and fragility of individual vocations. A group's vision grows and matures, but it can also wither and be lost. A community may abandon its dream, just as individual believers may allow their own religious hopes to die. When this happens in a parish, Sunday liturgies and special collections may continue, but the vision is gone. Members are exhorted rhetorically to follow the Gospel, but there is no longer any excitement or ambition to transform the world in the direction of the values of Christ.

As a faith community loses its vision, personal vocations wither. In the absence of a strong sense of corporate calling, without attractive examples of the Christian dream being lived out, individuals turn to other life ambitions. As a result, Christian values of love and justice penetrate less powerfully the fabric of their daily lives.

If a community can lose its dream, it can also allow it to narrow into a rigid and compulsive vision. This happens when a community seizes one aspect of Christian life (for example, personal piety or liturgical renewal or political action) and gives it exclusive and obsessive attention. In one group, then, being "born again" becomes the only acceptable credential of Christian holiness. Another, in its enthusiasm for protecting unborn children, neglects other concerns of Christian justice and mercy. Among others, the sense that the Church must "take a stand" on a politically sensitive issue closes them to the challenges or alternative insights of other Christians. Each of these dreams attempts to simplify the complex vision of Christian life. But doing so easily leads to a kind of idolatry: this partial vision is identified with God's will for everyone. A single action or conviction establishes one's orthodoxy and goodness. Antagonistic defense of "our vision" replaces a broader and more open pursuit of the elusive kingdom of God. A community's dream, like that of an individual, can become a tyranny. Like any tyranny or compulsion, such a dream is recognized by its rigidity and lack of freedom. Defending its narrowed vision of "what we must to do to be saved," it tends to neglect its own need for continual purification.

The shared dream of a parish or school or religious congregation is, thus, very much like a personal vocation. Fragile and in need of purification, the group's dream is continually being revealed to it. And like an individual vocation, a Christian community's dream is imbedded in a larger vision and hope: the dream of the kingdom of God.

The Dream of the Kingdom of God

The vocations of Jews and Christians are rooted in an inherited dream, formed by a vision that has been maturing for three thousand years and more. Abraham sensed that he was being invited to leave his ancestors' home in search of a new land and a different way of life. In his dream of this different future, our own religious ambitions were born. Hundreds of years later his descendants, having escaped from Egypt and now wandering in the Sinai Desert, would remember this dream of Abraham. Was it not the same God who had called Abraham to his search who now impelled them to the dream of a secure and prosperous homeland? In the aridity of the desert, this dream took the shape of "a good and broad land, a land flowing with milk and honey" (Exodus 3:8).

This dream of a land flowing with milk and honey seemed, at first, to be realized in the new land of Israel and the kingdom that David and Solomon ruled. But as social injustice and the abuse of power grew, as Israel's infidelities to Yahweh multiplied, it became clear that their collective dream was far from realized. It began to seem to some that the very greatness of their kings and the splendor of their state were distractions from this dream.

As Israel matured (through failure, conversion, and more failure—the usual path of maturity), prophets appeared to re-excite the people in their collective dream and to further nuance this hope. Isaiah and Jeremiah were especially insistent that this dream of an idyllic place "flowing with milk and honey" also include concern for the poor, the widowed, and even the stranger. Isaiah envisioned a society in which ritual sacrifices are replaced by care and justice:

> Remove the evil of your doings from
>   before my eyes;
> cease to do evil,
>   learn to do good;
> seek justice,
>   rescue the oppressed,
> defend the orphan,
>   plead for the widow.
>
> ISAIAH 1:16–17

In such a transformed society, people "shall beat their swords into plowshares, / and their spears into pruning hooks; / nation shall not lift up sword against nation, / neither shall they learn war any more" (Isaiah 2:4).

But the challenges of the early prophets and new dreams of Isaiah and Jeremiah went largely unheeded in Israel. Jerusalem was overrun by its enemies, and the Israelites were led into exile, their dreams shattered. In the second part of the Book of Isaiah, written during this period of captivity, a new and powerful dream is imagined: the vision of a servant of Yahweh, a savior who will heal and restore their freedom. Isaiah invites these exiles to dream again:

> Here is my servant, whom I uphold,
>   my chosen, in whom my soul delights;
> I have put my spirit upon him;
>   he will bring forth justice to the nations.

ISAIAH 42:1

The dream, begun in Abraham's ambition to find a new home and revived in the early Israelites' vision of a land flowing with milk and honey, was undergoing a powerful transformation. This collective hope could not be simply identified with a national state, nor could it exclude the poor or the foreigner. In their experience of the Exile, the Israelites were again forced to revise, to reenvision their shared dream. Would this future place of justice and love be more interior than exterior, a realm founded more on personal commitment than on territorial sovereignty?

In the New Testament, Jesus sees his own life as committed to this dream of the kingdom of God. His ministry begins with the announcement that "the kingdom of God has come near" (Mark 1:15). The urgency of personal change and conversion, so central to Jesus' concerns in the gospels, arises from the imminence of this kingdom.

If there is great ambiguity in the New Testament about the kingdom of God—Is it to happen only with the end of the world or is it already occurring in our lives?—we can see that Jesus' life and the gospels are centrally concerned with the realization of this shared dream. In an encounter with the followers of John the Baptist, when they inquire if Jesus is the messiah, the dreamed-of one, Jesus tells them to report to John what they have seen. "The blind receive their sight, the lame walk, the lepers are cleansed, the deaf hear, the dead are raised, the poor have good news brought to them" (Luke 7:22). These personal and social changes are signs of the kingdom; this is how we can recognize the realization of the dream in our own lives. Toward the close of Matthew's Gospel, we find Jesus telling his followers what actions will bring them into this kingdom. "I was hungry and you gave me food, I was thirsty and you gave me something to drink, I was a stranger and you welcomed me, I was naked and you gave me clothing, I was sick and you took care of me, I was in prison and you visited me..." (Matthew 25:35–36). These actions of justice and love, of caring for "one of the least of these," bring a person into the dreamed-of and hoped-for kingdom of God. In these gospel accounts of the kingdom, it is made clear that our own actions contribute to or frustrate the coming of God's kingdom.

The whole of the gospels may be seen as an account of Jesus joining his own life ambition to the dream of the kingdom. His own actions—compassionately healing some while accusing others of falseness and injustice; his intense involvement with others alternating with periods of retreat and quiet—are guided by a vision of a certain style of life. Concern for healing and personal change overshadowed an interest in a strict observance of the many laws of Jewish life. And life clearly had an urgency about it: God's kingdom is about to be realized, and we must change our lives, now, to fit God's ambition.

Despite his understanding of and enthusiasm for this dream of the kingdom, Jesus was himself surprised and even confused by its development. Though he came to Jerusalem sensing danger, it was only in the garden of olives that he saw how radically different were God's plans for him. Facing his own death, Jesus had to confront the frustration and failure of his life ambition and dream. His vision of many more years of healing and challenge, of strengthening his friends in this new way of life—this dream was being broken. His own dream for his life was being purified and revised by his Father. Quite naturally, he resisted. He struggled against his death and the shattering of his dream of how the kingdom was to be pursued. Yet in the end he came to trust the movement of his Father's dream, and he came to see that the dream he had been nourishing and following did not belong to him. His own life and ambition belonged, finally, to the larger dream of the kingdom of God, a dream always being realized in strange and surprising ways.

In Jesus' death, his earlier life ambition was lost. And in this loss and death, a new vision and dream began to live. The particular dream that would in time be called "Christian" began to grow. Its peculiarity is its convictions (reinforced in the personal experience of believers) that our dreams and careers and vocations are not our own and that it is by dying that they come to life. Christians understand their own life ambitions and visions as gifts, as more than their own possessions. Neither owning nor fully controlling our lives, we expect them to be changed, in unplanned and even painful ways, as we mature. The cross stands at the center of Christian faith and Christian dreaming—not out of morbidity but out of the realization that this is how we grow. Vocations and dreams rigidly adhered to become idols; ambitions too strongly defended, made invulnerable, are not Christian. Christian dreams, named for the person who most powerfully shapes our dreaming, expectably change as they are purified and come to match the dream that God is dreaming for us all.

The Story of Three Dreams

A Christian vocation may be described as a dream, God's dream for my life, developing in my imagination. Such a dream is gradually revealed to us in the various achievements and reversals of adult life. Since it is sometimes fragile, a personal vocation may be neglected and then wither. Or it may become compulsive and too well defended. Christian ministry always entails a fostering of dreams: clarifying and purifying our vocations, we come closer to imagining what God is about in our lives.

These personal dreams are imbedded in two levels of social life. They are rooted in the immediate contexts of our families and faith communities. And these groups have their own vocations—similarly frail but exciting. Christian maturing requires the interaction of dreams: our personal hopes in dialogue and in tension with our community's dreams and goals.

Both our individual vocations and our community's dreams are imbedded in the inherited hope for the kingdom of God. This ancient dream is both the beginning and end of Christian vocations. In Abraham's dream our vocations began; our best ambitions seek to make the kingdom come true. About any individual or community vocation we may ask, What does it have to do with the kingdom of God? Here we find the standard against which we judge the value of our dreams.

Christian maturing is thus an interplay of three dreams. In the mutual jostling, critique, and support of these three dreams we continue to uncover the purpose and possibility of our Christian life. Here, too, we see anew the place of the Church itself. No longer sensing itself the proud possessor of God's unambiguous plan for humankind, the Church guards a fragile and partial vision of God's dream for us. As a Church we have yet to imagine what God has in store for us. If this humbles us as an institution, it can also excite us: we are in the midst of a revelation. All the dreams have not been dreamed; the Church's vocation is still being revealed.

In his life, Jesus both proclaimed the coming of the kingdom and announced its location: "The kingdom of God is among you" (Luke 17:21). We might still ask, "Where is it among us?" The answer may be that it is in our imaginations. The dream of the kingdom of God is real because it already exists in us. It is frail and in need of nurturance because it exists mostly in our imaginations. This dream of God is not simply beyond us; if it were we could not even imagine it. It is within us, and not just in art individualistic fashion. The "you" of the New Testament statement is plural: the kingdom of God is stirring in our shared visions, in our community's ambitions and hopes. This is good news for communities of faith. Surviving the clash of different hopes and visions, we can still generate in our shared life that ancient dream of the kingdom of God. Pursuing our vocations, personal and corporate, we move this dream of God closer to its realization.

Reflective Exercise

Trace the maturing of your own dream and vocation by asking the following questions:

1. When did I first become aware of my ambition for my life? (Take time to return in your memory to explore the early shape of this dream.)
2. How have my best hopes for my life mellowed and changed over the past decade?
3. What is the most significant crisis that my dream and vocation have undergone? How was my dream threatened, or wounded, or purified in that crisis?

It may also be fruitful to explore the connections between your personal vocation and the social dreams that influence it.

1. What are the dreams or deepest hopes of the group that is most important in your life? (This may be your family or workplace or religious congregation.)
2. How does this corporate dream support or challenge your own vocation?

CHAPTER THREE

A Vocation Develops: Child to Disciple

C hild of God, disciple of the Lord, steward of the faith—
these are enduring images of Christian spirituality. Each
of these images, rooted in sacred Scripture and richly elaborated
in Christian piety, has helped shape the awareness of a Christian
vocation. Taken alone, each celebrates a central religious
conviction. Taken together, they suggest a pattern of spiritual
development that gives shape to Christian maturing. In this
chapter and the next, we place these images in a developmental
context, linking these movements of growth. The child of God
is meant to mature into the disciple but without leaving the
strengths of childhood behind. The disciple, already in an
important early stage of religious adulthood, is being readied
for new roles of stewardship in the community of faith. In this
more authoritative stage of stewardship, discipleship is not to
be abandoned but matured. The image of religious development
here is not a staircase of rigid roles but a spiral of widening
strengths: the child survives in the disciple, the disciple matures
and endures in the steward.

Child of God

We begin our lives, both biologically and religiously, as children. As children we know ourselves to be dependent, necessarily and properly so. We receive life and care from our parents; as Christians we confess a profound and unending dependence on God. This dependence is both a characteristic of childhood and one of its greatest strengths. Our maturing will require the expansion of this dependence as it ripens into the adult strengths of reliance and reliability. But, as we shall see later in this chapter, this expansion is a transformation of dependence rather than its abandonment.

It is in our early experiences of dependence as children that we first learn to trust the power of others. This foundational experience of dependence—of finding strength in others who are reliable in the face of our needs—is the first stage of the lifelong journey toward adult interdependence. Maturity invites us toward a complex dependability: we become strong enough for others to depend on us even as we remain able to depend on others, to trust their strength, to be vulnerable to those we love.

If dependence is the first characteristic of childhood, a second is playfulness. A child is essentially a player. In the free space of childhood, before the "serious business" of adult life overtakes us, we begin our play. Feeling the delight of our bodies and testing the limits in our environment, we "play" at life. The root of this play is imagination. In childhood, if we are fortunate, the extraordinary power of imagination begins to be flexed and developed within us. In play we are able to alter our world, to invent new playmates, to name—and in this way begin to befriend—some of the surprising forces arising within us. These two strengths of childhood, dependence and play, are important to maturity as well.

The Paradox of Childhood

Christians experience a peculiar paradox in their ambition to mature. We share the development described by Saint Paul.

When I was a child, I spoke like a child, I thought like a child, I reasoned like a child; when I became an adult, I put an end to childish ways.

1 CORINTHIANS 13:11

These "childish ways" are specified elsewhere in the Pauline letters. The child suffers the severe dependency of the slave (Galatians 4), and the child, without the experience to give him or her a sure sense of purpose, is necessarily "tossed to and fro and blown about by every wind of doctrine, by people's trickery, by their craftiness in deceitful scheming" (Ephesians 4:14).

Yet we know that childhood is not to be too thoroughly abandoned. We remember that provocative statement by Jesus that "unless you change and become like children, you will never enter the kingdom of heaven" (Matthew 18:3). A conversion is required for the recovery of childhood demanded for Christian maturing. How are we to outgrow childhood and simultaneously make our return?

We can approach this paradox by noting two temptations in the movement out of childhood: we may fail by leaving behind the strengths first experienced as a child or by refusing to accept the new strengths required of the adult. In the first temptation, the attempt is to escape dependency. In an eagerness to become an independent and able adult, I may shrug off every manner of dependence. I become "my own person," a full individualist. I wrench myself away from "childish" attachments to other people, those ambiguous ties that bind me both in love and control. Especially if I have experienced my childhood dependence as demeaning and manipulative, I am likely to be wary of adult intimacy and its commitments of affection and fidelity. Defensive and cautious about getting too close to others, I try to become strong enough to stand alone. Following this path of "mock maturity," I am also likely to abandon imagination and play. If, as in dependence, I identify these as childish, I must leave them behind in my trek into the gray sobriety of adult life. Thus the American stereotype: an adult who is serious and independent, an earnest achiever who can "go it alone," a "grown-up" in whom the child (and all its delights) has truly died.

But there is an opposite temptation in the movement beyond childhood—to cling to dependence too long. Frightened by the possibility of failure, I am reluctant to move beyond the secure realm where "other people know best." Or, unsure of my own ability, I am unwilling to set out on my own, afraid to test myself in the public realm. These are normal anxieties in the movement beyond adolescence. For some of us, however, the struggle overwhelms. Instead of gradually letting go of these dependencies of childhood, I hold on to them as the best defense against a confusing adult world. Here dependence, originally a childlike grace, becomes childish.

Religiously this is evidenced in the midlife Christian who, while responsible in family and career matters, remains overly dependent in religious affairs. Unable to depend on inner resources (which should, by now, have been tested and seasoned by several decades of adult experience), such an adult acts "like a child" in religious and moral areas.

This path of immaturity does not always result from personal failing alone. It is engendered and reinforced by institutions that have succumbed to the temptation of paternalism. Paternalism twists the compelling symbol of the family into a model of social control. Paternalism freezes the categories of parent and child: certain of us are seen as "parents" who care for (and control) others of us who are seen as—and must remain—children. The expectable movement of the child into adulthood, into a position of greater responsibility and author- ity for his own life, is frustrated or denied. Paternalism needs children; it thrives by enforcing a childish dependence, by re- quiring that its subjects remain children. Only when Christian institutions resist this temptation of paternalism are they able to support our religious maturing into adult children of God.

The Survival of the Child

The call to turn and become like children invites us to recover the strengths that we may have lost in an early adult pursuit of exaggerated independence. In the face of the American cultur- al commitment to independence, "to depend on others" often seems a negative experience. Relying on others is taken as a sign of weakness, a source of shame. But most of us sense the limitations of this cultural embarrassment over needing other people. To have in our lives others on whom we can depend— as children, we may have taken this for granted. As adults, we are more sensitive to the significance of such dependable friends. We cherish such relationships as special and rare. And we be- come more aware of the strength that such dependence requires. To come to trust others, I must allow myself to be vulnerable to them. To accept the gift of your love, I must be strong enough to admit that I need you. As adults we come to know that this kind of openness demands much of us. But its risks are richly rewarded. Our commitments of love and work demand the strength of dependence. The child's ability to depend, matured by the experiences of the twenties and thirties, is transformed as an adult strength. No longer a childish dependence, it re- mains a resource linked to the child within us.

Similarly, after a decade or more devoted to serious adult achievement, we may begin to rediscover our earlier playful- ness. Sometimes this adult play is interpreted as regression; more often it is an expansion of maturity. In adult play we salute the child in us, giving spontaneity and delight a place in our lives again. The responsibilities and duties of adult life can easily banish the child in us, and we feel the effects of this loss. In experiences of play and in new modes of adult dependence, we allow the child to survive and to contribute to our adult lives.

For Christians the survival of the child has religious significance as well. All our lives we remain children of God—dependent on the Creator's love, heirs to the kingdom of God. Yet the children of God must mature as adult Christians. As adult offspring in the family of God, we develop into active collaborators in family decisions. An early stage of this journey into religious adulthood is experienced in the call to discipleship.

Disciples of the Lord

As we move beyond adolescence into young adult life, we make those choices which signal a new stage of maturity. In our initial commitments of love and work we manifest our hopes, test our values, and begin to define our adult responsibilities. Religiously, we might describe this first stage of adult maturing as a period of discipleship.

The word *disciple* is so thoroughly a part of Christian rhetoric that its developmental sense is easily lost. We will focus here on several practical characteristics of this stage of maturity. The move into adulthood is marked by its decisions: I choose to pursue this career path; I initiate this relationship; I select this lifestyle for myself. There is often a tentativeness about those choices, but they are, nonetheless, personal choices. To be an adult is to be able to, to have to, make these kinds of decisions.

The inner reality of these decisions is complex. These are movements of personal choice experienced as responses. I choose a vocation because I feel called to it. My love for you is as much a response to your lovableness as it is a decision on my part. I move toward a career that seems to hold promise. The young adult experiences these early commitments—in vocation, in relationship, in career—as a mutual pledge.

To be a disciple is to experience myself as religiously decisive. I must choose to follow Jesus Christ. I choose to be a Christian rather than simply continuing to attend the church of my parents or friends. Here again, the experience of the mutuality of the pledge is important. I am aware that I can choose the Lord only because I have first been chosen. I sense that my adult faith is a gift; my own choice can be made only in response. Some of us experience this movement into religious discipleship in our late teens or early twenties as part of a young adult conversion or vocational choice. But for many, a moratorium intervenes between the child and the disciple. Leaving behind the simplicity and even naivete of their childlike faith, these young adults do not directly enter a period of discipleship. Their twenties become a time-in-between, a moratorium when they are no longer children but not yet Christian adults. For some, then, it is not until their thirties or later that they decisively involve themselves in the Christian faith. It may be a family crisis that reawakens deeper questions of religious meaning. Or a concern for their children's awareness of religious and moral values. Experiences with the Rite of Christian Initiation of Adults in the parish may lead them to a mature appreciation of religious commitment. Or participation in parish renewal or Cursillo or Marriage Encounter moves them to choose a more adult stance of Christian faith. Whether in the teens or in midlife, discipleship begins in an adult decision to follow Christ.

The disciple is an adult who both initiates and follows. The word *disciple* itself means a learner. The cultural equivalent is an apprentice. In our first jobs most of us experience ourselves as learners and apprentices. Whether in an agency or a parish, as a plumber or a teacher, there is much that we have to learn "on the job." New to adult responsibilities, we are still learning from those with more experience. This dependence on external authority is proper to young adult life. As beginning ministers or carpenters or nurses, we find ourselves asking, "How do we do it around here?" For guidance we look to other people's experience and expertise as we struggle to "get it right."

Even in our commitments of intimacy we begin as apprentices. In the first years of marriage, many young couples define their relationship from the outside, either imitating other marriages or resisting doing so. Only gradually do they grow into a confident sense of what their own marriage requires. The person who enters a vowed religious life goes through a period of formal apprenticeship in which the titles themselves—candidate, novice, junior—designate the process as one of discipleship. Already capable adults, through our twenties we are still learning how the interplay of society's expectations and our own deepest hopes will shape our careers and vocations. Over the first decades of adult life, our instincts and intuitions continue to mature as they are challenged by new experiences, shaped by our hopes for the future, and expressed in the decisions we make.

In our religious discipleship we apprentice ourselves to Jesus Christ. We take the posture of listeners and learners to the Scripture, to the Church, to a spiritual guide. The special quality of religious learning that goes on during this time is captured in a word that shares the same root as disciple: discipline. The learner's stance has the disciple look outward, toward objective sources of truth that have proven themselves authoritative. External criteria are important. I test myself against these values to see if I can "measure up." I try to match my life and performance to that of worthy models. I attempt to hold my experiences, hopes, and decisions accountable to the values and hopes of Jesus Christ. Thus the disciple is open to influence: I want to be shaped by the power to which I apprentice myself. It is transformation that I seek.

The effect of this transformation is the internalization of these values and hopes; they now become a part of me. Discipleship starts in chosen dependence on an outside authority. But its goal is that I become less dependent on external criteria, as my inner resources become more available and more reliable.

The discipline involved in this gradual transformation is a seasoning of instincts. Over many seasons the values of the Gospel slowly shape our sensibilities about love and commitment, about work and success, about power and justice. As I experience this seasoning, I gradually become more confident in acknowledging my insights and intuitions. Now disciplined, they can be followed. The disciple matures as these instincts become increasingly trustworthy. This developing inner resource (described more traditionally as mature adult conscience) will be a crucial part of the person's future stewardship.

As the locus of personal authority begins to move within, I experience the fruits of discipleship—commitment and fidelity. It is as my inner resources become more reliable that I become capable of adult commitment. I develop the emotional and intellectual strength required to establish—and to maintain—bonds that pledge my future. My fidelity becomes more resilient. Less "scandalized" by the inconsistencies I find in myself and others—and even in the Church—I am able to reaffirm the values of love and justice, of reconciliation and peace, that we hold as a community of faith, even when it seems they are present among us more in hope than in truth. I grow flexible enough to be truly faithful, able—in the words of Erik Erikson—"to sustain loyalties freely pledged in spite of the inevitable contradictions of value systems." Such are the strengths the disciple must take into stewardship.

The Role of the Mentor

For many of us, our own experience of discipleship includes a relationship with a mentor. A mentor is someone to whom I can apprentice myself—a teacher or supervisor, an older member of the congregation, the principal or pastor in my first ministry. The mentor is not a parent but a more experienced adult who fosters my growth into adult competence. Mature mentoring—an instance of nonmanipulative adult care—can heal our adolescent biases against dependency and authority. We find we can rely on others in an adult way that is not demeaning. The authority of the mentor is not an authority "over me," but an authority that urges me to believe more in myself.

The process of discipleship can be frustrated when a mentor is lacking. With no particular person to encourage and challenge me, "following Christ" can become too private a journey —an experience without practical accountability. Ministry to those in discipleship in our parishes and communities will mean, among other things, providing such mature mentors.

The New Testament shows us Jesus in the role of mentor. Mark's Gospel (6:7–13) reports Jesus' words to his disciples as he sends them out to preach and heal. His instructions give hints of what is required of discipleship today. Jesus tells his followers to travel light, to go with a companion, and to be ready to move on.

To travel light is to resist the cultural baggage, the accumulated expectations of adult life. "Light" also suggests less seriousness, less gravity about what we do. Jesus tells the disciples to travel together. Perhaps this is to remind us that companionship and interdependence mark his followers. This may go counter to some recent images of ministry that seem to demand a self-sufficiency able to "go it alone," the kind of person who is available to give but never open to receive in return. Such a minister may well travel light, but always travels alone. Traveling together witnesses to the communal quality of the life of faith; it also gives us someone to play with along the way.

Finally, Jesus encourages his disciples to be ready to move on, not to overinvest in any one place or effort. We are called to give our best effort to the tasks of ministry but always to be ready to move on. Delivered of a final responsibility, we can be a bit less grim and self-serious in our work. We are, after all, disciples of a master who calls us both to work in the vineyard and to play before him in his sight.

Temptations of Discipleship

If there are temptations characteristic of the child, there are specific temptations for the disciple as well. One of these arises from the very nature of discipleship: the earnestness that is part of being a learner. The disciple, like the apprentice, wants very much to do well. Intensely focused on our task (whether this is success in our career or growth in our spirituality), we are likely to be terrified by the possibility of failure. Error and mistakes appear to us as threats to our life ambition. Many adults report that the self-seriousness of this discipleship period, with its attendant fear of failure, left them unimaginative and without a sense of play. Only later would these childlike resources return, as part of a movement of maturity in mid-life.

A second temptation for the disciple arises in the challenge to mature. Secure as an apprentice, I may linger here too long. The learner's role is somewhat safe: I am not the one responsible. Others know better, there is more for me to learn, I am not yet ready to be in charge. I may settle for the shelter of being "only a beginner." But the increased demands that accompany the journey through our thirties and forties call us toward a new stage of religious maturity and a new level of service in the Christian community.

Comfortable as a follower, and grateful for the luxury of having others make the final decisions, the disciple may resist new invitations to leadership and greater responsibility. And, again, it is not personal insecurity alone that tempts the disciple to remain in this protected place. There are political advantages to be gained in an image of the Church that expects most of its members to remain lifelong in the position of followers.

Discipleship matures in us as our adult experience grows and our work responsibility increases. We find ourselves in more authoritative positions. The question that as disciples we asked—How do we do it around here?—is now addressed to us. We may feel uneasy in the awareness that others now look to us for direction. Yet amid the discomfort, we may also sense that it is time; we are ready for this kind of leadership. Our own continuing discipleship is maturing into a new shape. It will soon demand a new name, that of stewardship.

Reflective Exercise

Consider your own experience of discipleship.

1. Recall the adult choices of faith that have been part of your life:
   - experiences in which you have chosen to follow Christ.
   - decisions you have made to live as a Christian.
   - choices to participate in the life of the Church.
2. Explore the shape of your discipleship:
   - how have you been a listener and a learner in faith?
   - who are your religious mentors, those who have nurtured your movement into adult faith?
   - what are the strengths of your discipleship today?

3. Have you experienced the temptations of the disciple:
   - becoming overly serious, with the danger of losing touch with the child within?
   - clinging to the comfort of the learner's role?
   - refusing to take up the tasks of stewardship?

CHAPTER FOUR

A Vocation Matures: The Emergence of Stewardship

A t once children of God and disciples of the Lord, we continue to "put on Christ," to develop in the ways of Christian adulthood. In this movement of religious maturing, once fragile strengths are transformed into resilient virtues. As our vocations are seasoned, we move toward a new stage of life. Even as we remain followers of Jesus Christ, our discipleship takes new shape. With grace and good fortune, we become stewards.

The transformation of the disciple into the steward happens in diverse and sometimes subtle ways. For many Christians the transition begins in the late thirties or forties. An external event may trigger the change, perhaps a new assignment in ministry or a promotion in one's responsibility at work. The triggering event may be within the family, as parents realize that it is they who must decide about their children's religious education. Or the impetus toward stewardship may be more interior: I sense

I must begin to take my own religious experience more seriously, or I feel a need to be a more active contributor to the future of this religious congregation.

Whether the impulse is external or internal, the movement toward stewardship is recognized in a surge of responsibility and personal authority. We find we are called to trust ourselves in new and, perhaps, frightening ways. Formerly we could turn to others to ask, "What's the best way to do it?" Now, more experienced and in positions of greater responsibility, we realize we must turn more to our inner resources in making important decisions. If we are frightened by this increased responsibility—How do I know I will make the right decision?—we are also consoled by the increasing authority of our own experience, accumulated and tested over the past several decades. During our years of discipleship, we have been learning how to care well for others, how to express both our affection and our anger, how to act justly. We find that we have become more dependable. This increased personal authority and dependability means that we are now more than followers; we are becoming stewards.

Stewards differ from disciples in sensing the trustworthiness of their inner resources and the reliability of their convictions. The steward, of course, continues to be a disciple: this internal authority continues to be complemented and challenged by the authority of Scripture and the Church. But the central characteristic of stewardship is the ability to trust the authority of one's own maturing convictions.

This surge of responsibility and authority is matched by a paradoxical realization: as stewards we are responsible for what we do not own. Invited in midlife into more responsible jobs and more authoritative positions, we are reminded that what we care for—children, schools, parishes, the land—we do not ultimately possess. A steward is, by definition, not an owner. When Christian faith takes root in us, we recognize that creation and all its fruits belong to the Lord. Yet adult responsibility calls us to be assertive and decisive in our care for this creation. The challenge is to be caring without controlling, to be decisive without becoming possessive. The temptation we experience here is the one that accompanies any investment: when we care deeply for something we are inclined to try to control it, to possess it. Being a parent can initiate this discipline of stewardship. Gradually, sometimes painfully, parents must come to acknowledge that their children are not, in any final sense, "theirs." They are neither reproductions nor possessions. But it is not only by being a parent that adults are taught the lessons of stewardship. If we are fortunate, we also learn these in our jobs and projects and other "investments." Midlife maturing—its name is stewardship—entails a continuing purification of our care and decisiveness. We become able to sustain our investment in what we do not possess.

Stewardship in Scripture

The paradox of nonpossessive care has a long tradition among Jews and Christians. It is rooted in our most basic relationship with our Creator. The writer of Psalm 39, impressed with the brevity and fragility of human life, expressed this relationship most powerfully: "I am your guest and only for a time, a nomad like all my ancestors" (JB). This sense of belonging in a world that we do not own becomes, in our better moments, our religious sense of identity. This "guest involvement" describes a Christian steward today: parents discover that they are guest parents; a pastor is always a guest pastor. Every adult expression of responsibility and authority is recognized as a guest performance. That we fail at this more often than we succeed only reminds us that stewardship is an extraordinary ideal that demands a severe maturity.

The word *steward* appears in the gospels only in Luke's account, and then only at two points. The first appearance is the famous parable of the faithful steward (Luke 12). This story highlights three features of a steward. The steward acts as a servant rather than as an owner or ruler. The main strength of a steward is a combination of wisdom and trustworthiness— an experienced dependability. The context of stewardship is absence—the steward acts in the absence of the master. The second appearance of the steward in Luke is in the story of the unjust steward who, about to be fired, is astute enough to reduce what his master's debtors owe (Luke 16). Again the steward acts with a certain wisdom or astuteness, on his own authority and in the absence of the master.

Saint Paul, in his First Letter to the Corinthians, describes the same characteristics of the steward: such a person acts as a servant, is trustworthy, and performs in the absence of the master—"before the Lord comes" (4:5).

The role of servant is meant to deprive the steward of independence and possessiveness. The virtue of trustworthiness points to a reliability, an inner authority that has developed "on the job" and on which the steward can depend. The third characteristic is more complex and perhaps frightening: the context of stewardship is absence. The authority of stewards arises both from their trustworthiness and from the absence of their master.

Stewards in Absence

The absence of Jesus Christ, begun in his traumatic death and celebrated in his ascension, is the context of Christian stewardship. In his death Jesus absented himself from the community. This abnegation had startling results: it brought the Spirit into our midst in new and stirring ways, and it lured us into more authoritative roles in our shared life. In the presence of Jesus we had but to follow; we had a leader possessed of God like no other. When the Lord is present, we are all fittingly disciples. In the "generous absence" of Jesus Christ a space was created, a leadership vacuum generated. Jesus' absence invokes our stewardship.

To be sure, Christ is not gone forever. The Lord is among us, present in the Spirit and in the community gathered in his name. But if we really believe in the Second Coming—the culmination of human stewardship—we must believe in Christ's absence now. We must learn to honor that absence. Our willingness to become stewards is one of the significant ways in which we honor the Lord's absence.

Developmentally, absence seems to have an important role in every kind of leadership and adult maturing. In our forties—expectably the first full season of stewardship—we come into a new intimacy with absence. Our parents are aging and approaching death. We are likely to have experienced the death of a friend or colleague and to have mourned this kind of loss. Mentors and leaders once so compelling and directive in our lives are less present. We taste absence in a new way in midlife as we are gradually but surely orphaned. But this loss of parents and mentors creates the space for our own authority and leadership. Absence is the empty but fertile soil in which our midlife authority is compelled to grow.

But such absence is frightening, and Christian tradition has been tempted to disguise it. One strategy for avoiding this absence is paternalism. Paternalism substitutes a simplified world of parents and children for the complex adult world of shared responsibility, conflict, and negotiation. A paternalistic Church divides its believers, rigidly, between parents and children. It then provides "paternal" ministers (whether named "father" or not) to preside over a "childlike" laity. The exciting and graceful image of the family is thus distorted in the static dichotomy of clergy and laity. The laity are guaranteed care; they need never confront the absence of the Lord. But the costs of this care are high.

A new awareness of the adult nature of Christian faith, reawakened in Vatican II, has alerted us to the limits of family imagery. In its warmth and intimacy, the metaphor of the family can be used to prolong our childhood. If family is the only image we have of our life together as believers, we can fall victim to the subtle shift from knowing ourselves to be children of God to acting as children toward church leaders. Paternalism improperly fills the gap of Christ's absence. It makes present to us "other christs" who would parent us in faith. But this strategy, we are coming to see, does not honor absence. Either frightened by absence or fearing its implications (the demand that adult Christians come to trust their own consciences and act with the authority of stewards), we can let paternalism distract us from this pregnant absence.

Stewards of Our Faith

To be a steward is to be authoritatively involved in the Christian faith. More than a child or a disciple, a steward is responsible for handing on this faith. Special challenges of stewardship are being felt today in two central areas of Christian life: Scripture and liturgy. We are all disciples of Scripture. Whatever our education or maturity or ministerial role, we continue throughout our lives as learners before this sacred text. Our lives are interpreted by Scripture. Ideally, from childhood on we are apprenticed to these texts, learning their imagery, experiencing their complex and profound influence. Disciples of the Scripture in these ways, we are gradually invited to become stewards of the Scripture as well. A steward assumes a more authoritative attitude toward the sacred text. Responsible for handing on the faith in our communities, we become—necessarily—interpreters of Scripture. We select certain images from Scripture for special emphasis, we call attention to the contemporary significance of a biblical story that goes beyond its conventional understanding, we arrange passages in an attempt to hand on their revelation more gracefully. As stewards, then, we stand in that precarious position of being both interpreted by God's Word and interpreting it. In every age, Christians have chosen for emphasis the scriptural passages that will influence their lives; the steward is someone who does so with an experienced sense of caution and confidence.

Guided by our Scriptures, we Christians celebrate God's presence in the liturgy. Here, too, we can trace a maturing of discipleship toward stewardship. As disciples we participate in the Church's worship: we attend the liturgy, following the lead of the celebrant. Catholics especially have had a rather severe distinction between disciples and stewards in regard to the Eucharist. In years past, the altar railing stood as the clear barrier between the steward who was "saying Mass" and the disciples in attendance. In most of our churches the altar railing is gone, allowing for greater mobility at the liturgy. Parishioners come up to offer the readings; a variety of ministers distributes communion. With more members of the community sharing in the planning of the Eucharist, liturgical stewardship is expanding. The steward of the liturgy differs from the disciple not in excellence but by the mode of participation. Christian stewards—lay and ordained—*initiate* the liturgy in some way: in selecting the readings, in planning the music, in giving the homily, in presiding.

Throughout the Catholic Church more adult believers are coming forward to complement the traditional, sacramental stewardship of the ordained priest. In parishes in South America, in a priest's absence lay leaders celebrate the presence of the Lord in the community. In congregations of women religious, stewards within the community are imaginatively designing communion services and other liturgies in the absence of a more traditional chaplain. More and more lay parish life coordinators assume administrative roles where resident priests are absent. Small groups of lay Catholics are celebrating the presence of the Lord in their homes—not in defiance but as an expansion of the parish's liturgical life. In all these instances, as well as in the greater sharing of the planning and presiding at parish worship, Christian liturgical stewardship continues to blossom. The changes that this portends in Catholic liturgical practice are great. Without doubt, some efforts to re-imagine liturgical stewardship may include excess and immaturity. Growth seems seldom to be achieved without embarrassment and even error along the way. More impressive, however, is the potential maturing of the adult worshiping community as its members come to a more assertive sense of their responsibility and authority regarding this central exercise of the faith.

Stewardship appears in our life as our discipleship leads us toward new responsibilities and greater personal authority. But we do not experience these invitations of religious maturity in a social vacuum. The structures of our families and our churches can foster this religious development or frustrate it. A young woman, the oldest of several children, may be forced into an early role as steward in her family by the untimely death of her parents. A recently ordained priest may be thrust into great pastoral responsibility at an early age. Such premature demands for stewardship sometimes provoke an early maturity. Often, however, they lead to exhaustion. In midlife these early stewards may yearn for an experience as learner and follower, for the leisure of a "lost discipleship."

And the reverse of this premature stewardship is likely to occur as well. A woman religious, matured by several decades of service, is ready for wider diocesan leadership. But the diocese may not be ready for her. Its structures may not be prepared to welcome stewardship in a woman of such experience. Or a midlife layman, eager to contribute to his parish, can find no way to express this ambition and readiness. A narrow interpretation of parish stewardship leaves no room for a shared leadership. The Church, as God's handiwork, is meant to foster our religious growth; as a human institution it often enough imposes barriers to our maturing, just as we ourselves tend to restrict our role in ministry. An expanded sense of stewardship will require a purification of both ourselves and church structures.

The growth of discipleship into stewardship includes a shifting sense of responsibility to one's religious heritage. The disciple is one who ministers from within the Christian tradition, grounded in and shaped by it. The steward is also able to minister to the tradition itself. Disciples are still learning about the best of our heritage as a believing people; stewards have matured to the point where they are able to, and need to, care for the worst of religious heritage. As disciples of the Church we begin to care for the wounds of the world; as more experienced stewards we must also come to care for the wounds of the Church.

Such a stewardship arises from a certain vision of the Church. The Christian Church, as graced as it is with God's enduring presence, is also the wounded and scarred body of Christ. Human as well as divine, the Church is sometimes sinful, often immature, and in many ways grievously wounded. Some of these wounds are self-inflicted, appearing in the gaps between our high ideals and our halting practice. Who will minister to these wounds in the body of Christ? Children of God are not strong enough to do so; disciples are not yet sufficiently experienced or hardy for the task. It is the stewards, tested and strengthened by decades of adult Christian living, who are strong enough in faith to take up the task of carefully and patiently binding up the Church's wounds. Such a role demands extraordinary maturity and a deep awareness of one's own woundedness. Yet this is the stuff of Christian stewardship.

Just as children of God and disciples experience certain temptations, stewards are typically tempted in particular ways as well. The central danger of this stage of Christian service is possessiveness. Involved in responsible choices and authoritative decisions in the community, stewards may forget they are servants. The community or parish or diocese comes to be seen as "theirs." An arrogant or defensive "I'm in charge here" replaces the more open and responsive posture of the steward. Thus the need for the special discipline of this stage of leadership: to recall, again and again, that our authority is a guest responsibility, a gift to be exercised for a short time in the service of the Lord.

A second threat to the exercise of stewardship is seen in the Christian leader who is unable to let go. Accustomed to leadership and its perquisites, a steward may find it difficult to give these up, to step aside, to hand over leadership to the next generation. Clinging to the status or protection of their authority, such stewards contend that the next generation is not yet ready for leadership. And, of course, from the sagacious position of those of us currently in charge, the next generation is, almost by definition, never ready. Its members do not have our experience or our savvy or our plain good sense. They have not lived our lives. Worst, they are not us. But they are the future. And it is in overcoming this temptation of stewardship, in learning to share with the next generation the control of the world that will be theirs more than ours, that our stewardship makes its richest contribution.

The Interplay of Child, Disciple, Steward

Perhaps the most important feature of this understanding of Christian maturing is the continuing interplay and the survival of all three aspects of our religious life. As we mature into adult discipleship, we ought not leave all of childhood behind. To fully abandon childhood means to lose our ability to be dependent and imaginative and playful as adults. And we know from experience how often this happens. The earnestness with which we pursue our careers and other commitments commonly leaves us competent but unplayful. In becoming "successful" in our adult responsibilities, we may become wary of the interdependence required for adult commitments. How are we to become (in Erik Erikson's phrase) "independent enough to be dependable"? How can we learn to combine an adult sense of responsibility with a playful imagination? These are the challenges we face as disciples.

As we mature into stewardship—whether in regard to our communities or our career or the Church—we are reminded that we continue to be disciples. As followers of Jesus Christ, we remain apprenticed for a lifetime. We must always remain learners as well. We sense the illusion involved in the person who considers himself so learned that he need not listen any longer, so authoritative that he need not learn from anyone else. We recognize here the distortion of a stewardship that severs itself from a continuing discipleship.

Religious maturing involves us in the interplay of child, disciple, and steward. Our earlier reminder bears repeating here: the image that captures this movement best is not that of successive stair steps but of an expanding spiral. The goal of growth into discipleship is not to leave behind the strengths of the child but to enlarge these. The movement into stewardship is not meant to be a repudiation of the strengths of the disciple but an expansion of these.

One of the intriguing aspects of this interplay is the connection between stewardship and the return of the strengths of the child. Many of us have sensed, in the movements of our own maturing in ministry, the loss of the child along the way. The earnestness of our twenties and thirties left us little time or tolerance for play. Imagination was gradually abandoned in the seriousness of young adulthood. Many in ministry report that it was with the advent of stewardship in their lives—the movement into a more responsible job or the development of a more confident sense of personal authority—that the child surprisingly returned. An important connection between stewardship and the strengths of the child is a comfort with error.

Several decades of adult living give us experience with failure. We come to learn that mistakes and errors are unavoidable and do not, in fact, destroy us. This insight not only prepares us to be more tolerant of others but allows the child to return in our own lives. Stewards, like children, can take more risks because they are able to laugh at their mistakes. This freedom seems to release resources of both courage and creativity. The "seriousness" of the disciple is lifted, and we become both more authoritative stewards and more imaginative and childlike.

And the second characteristic of childhood—dependence— is also involved in the advent of stewardship. In our young adult years, many of us struggle toward a satisfying indepen- dence. We are still busy letting go of a dependency on parents that no longer fits; we may be wary of new dependencies, wheth- er in work or in love. But, as we noted in the last chapter, maturity can make us more "dependable" in both senses of the word. We become reliable, strong enough for others to be able to depend on us. And we become better at depending on others. We have learned that such dependencies need not en- slave or belittle us. After the earnest seriousness of our twen- ties and thirties, the emergency of stewardship may include the surprising recovery of these gifts of the child within us. Now more capable of being both imaginative and faithful followers, we are better able to contribute to shaping the community of faith for the future.

Reflective Exercise

Recall your experience in the community of faith over the past several years, alert for signs of your own movement into stew- ardship.

The stimulus may have been from the outside—moving into greater responsibility in your work or experiencing new de- mands as a result of changes in the family.

Or there may have been a more internal source—a decision that forced you to trust your own instincts or a shift in your sense of yourself as an adult.

Spend some time now with these memories, letting the experience of your own movement in stewardship become alive for you again. Then consider these questions:

1. What strengths have you experienced in your movement into stewardship?
2. For you, what risks have been involved in becoming a steward?
3. How is discipleship part of your stewardship today?
4. In what ways does the child survive as part of your own religious maturity?

CHAPTER FIVE

The Seasoning
of Senses

C hristian maturing is neither exotic nor magical. It takes
shape in the critical choices and decisions by which we
fashion our lives. I choose to marry this person; I decide to
change jobs; I resolve to commit myself to this effort of social
reform. A dozen or so major life choices are bound together
and expressed in scores of daily judgments. These decisions,
over decades, provide a specific pattern to our life, giving it
both its uniqueness and its special Christian flavor.

How do we come to these decisions? What guides us toward good and fruitful choices? We know there is more here
than clear rational decisions based on objective information.
Critical choices entail more than a stiff dose of willpower that
"makes" us do the right thing. These choices and decisions
depend, finally, on trustworthy instincts, on feelings that have
become reliable. We "sense" that this commitment or change
is the proper choice. In this chapter we wish to trace the maturing of our senses as they become reliable resources in Christian life.

Emotions, intuitions, instincts—these are disconcerting words for many Christians. Is not religious faith that gift of personal conviction that rescues us from the tumult of feeling? Is not Christian belief a certainty that liberates us from the moods and impulses that sometimes threaten to overturn our lives? We may have learned that faith is an intellectual assent, an act of the mind that does not depend on volatile and changing emotions. Or we may have been taught that moral choice is a movement of willpower: Christians are meant to make hard choices about what they "ought to do" and not be led astray by what they "feel like doing." Often enough, what may start as a healthy hesitance about feelings leads to a less healthy mistrust of them. No longer our friends, our feelings are neglected or suppressed. And when they return, they come to punish.

Part of the Christian renaissance occurring these days is a renewed optimism about human feelings. Affection, anger, consolation, confusion, joy—these are expressions of the human spirit. We are more aware today that these emotions are part of the life of the Spirit as well. With reawakened respect for these powerful resources, Christians today are trying to understand better how our feelings are a part of our maturing into "the fullness of Christ."

In Christian spirituality there is an increasing attention given to discernment, the process by which we come to wise decisions in the important questions in our life. These critical questions—Is it time to leave this job? Should we have another child? What direction does my priesthood take now?—are always matters upon which we must act "before all the facts are in." We decide, often with trepidation, guided by intuition and by a gradually more confident "sense" of how we are to act. At the heart of this discernment is the gradual process that refines our feelings and renders our instincts trustworthy. Graceful Christian living depends on the education of desire. Our hunches become wise in repeated purification; they may even become holy.

Christian liturgical life nurtures this purification. Here our emotions are shaped by prayer and movement, by costume and incense. Thus shaped, they can guide and enhance our celebration of God's presence among us. Liturgy is a school of the senses. In worship we recall Jesus' delight and anger and sorrow. We remember and celebrate his sense of when to confront others, when to heal, when to retreat. And the ritual movement of the liturgy is meant to shape us as well, forming our feelings so that they may display something of the power and nuance of Jesus' emotions.

The "Sense" of Scripture

In an effort to trace the maturing of emotion we turn to Scripture. The language of sense and feeling appears throughout the New Testament. But a deep-seated ambivalence about human feelings permeates Christian awareness. Is it not emotion that sweeps us away in acts of passion and sin? We can note this ambivalence in the English translations that disguise the seasoning of senses revealed in the gospel accounts.

In the New Testament the Greek word *phronein* means "to sense, to judge, to intuit." In some contexts it means "to be sensible"—to have a somewhat matured sense of how to act. And the same word may mean "to be prudent"—to have a refined sense of what action is proper. This single word, then, suggests changing levels of feeling: from sensation to sensibility to prudence. (In Aristotle's discussion of human virtue, this notion is translated as "practical wisdom.")

In the Latin translation of the New Testament this suggested pattern of our maturing senses is retained by the use of the word *sapere*. Meaning both "to sense" and "to be sensible," this is also the root of the word *sapientia*, wisdom. The suggestion is that wisdom is not a purely intellectual virtue but a matter of matured sensibilities. A look at some appearances of this word in the New Testament may give us a better vision of Christian maturing.

This word for "Christian sensibility" occurs in a number of interesting contexts. In the famous story of the ten young women awaiting the bridegroom, we find that five are foolish (not having brought enough oil for their lamps to outlast the tardy arrival of the groom) and that five are "wise" or "sensible" (Matthew 25). The latter five had the good wit or judgment or prudence to bring some extra oil, just in case.

A stranger use of this term appears in Jesus' commissioning of his disciples. As he sends them out into the world, he encourages them to be "wise as serpents and innocent as doves" (Matthew 10:16). The highly developed instincts of a snake, its cunning, is described by this same word, *phronein*.

We find another surprising use of this term in the story of the dishonest steward (Luke 16). About to be fired by his employer, he makes friends with his employer's debtors by reducing their obligations. His employer goes on to fire him, but with praise for his "astuteness." In a crisis, he had the "good sense" or astuteness to act a certain way. Prudent young women, a cunning snake, an astute (if dishonest) steward—each displays a certain developed judgment, a sense of what to do in a special situation.

A much more instructive use of this word occurs in the story of the disciples' reaction to Jesus' decision to go to Jerusalem, even if it meant his death (Matthew 16; Mark 8). Jesus has decided that he must go to the capital to confront the authorities; it is time to act. Peter strongly objects to this plan. The two men clearly have very different feelings about what is to be done. Jesus, suddenly angered, utters one of his most emphatic statements: Get behind me, Satan! You are an obstacle in my path, because you do not *sense* the things of God, but those of humans (see Matthew 16:23). Peter's way of feeling— his instinctive response that Jesus ought not to take the chance of going to Jerusalem, ought not to follow this inner urging which could make him vulnerable to death—is opposed to "feeling the things of God." Peter has followed his feelings and instincts, but the wrong ones. He has responded in a seemingly sensible fashion, but in a way that Jesus finds unholy. In his decision to go to Jerusalem, Jesus is following his own instincts and sense, but it is also "the sense of God," a sense of how he is to act that has been formed by his attentiveness to his father.

This important opposition of feelings, of ways of judging, can be easily lost for the English reader of the Scriptures. In many translations the feeling tone of *phronein* is hidden beneath more cognitive renditions. In the *New Revised Standard Version* the above phrase in Matthew 16:23 is translated as "for you are setting your mind not on divine things but on human things." In the *Oxford Revised Standard* translation, all sensing disappears in "you are not on the side of God, but of men." When we return some "feeling" to this passage, we better recognize Jesus' insistence on "a godly way of sensing" that is quite different from our more ordinary sensibilities. And this may help us as we scrutinize our own difficult decisions. As I come to an important life choice, I examine the feelings and instincts that are leading me to this choice. Does this growing "sense" of what I should do arise from selfishness or cowardice? Or is it rooted in an attentive listening to God's guidance in my life? An important moment in religious maturity comes in my recognition of the trustworthiness of my feelings. Purified in innumerable trials and errors, my senses have become more reliable. This is the gradually accrued confidence, developed over decades of Christian living, that I can trust my senses because they are of God.

A second passage that distinguishes a mature Christian way of sensing appears at the end of Paul's First Letter to the Corinthians. Describing the different stages of religious maturity, Paul turns to the metaphor of human development: When I was a child, I used to talk like a child, *feel* like a child, and argue like a child, but now I am an adult, all childish ways are put behind me (see 13:11).

Again we encounter an opposition of ways of behaving, rooted in ways of feeling. Adult maturity entails the letting go of childish ways of feeling or, more accurately, the transformation of these ways of feeling as they become more trustworthy resources.

Again, a "way of feeling" is disguised in many English translations. Both the *Jerusalem Bible* and the *Oxford Revised Standard* translate this phrase as "to think like a child." By restoring some "feeling" to this passage, we can recover the early Christian awareness that religious maturity is very much concerned with feelings and sense.

One of Paul's most emphatic statements about Christian feelings appears in his Letter to the Romans. Paul makes the famous distinction between those who live according to the flesh and those who live according to the Spirit (8:5). The first "set their minds on the things of the flesh," while the others "set their minds on the things of the Spirit." "Set their minds" is the translation of the *Oxford Revised Standard* and the *New Revised Standard Version*; again the feeling aspect of this personal inclination is disguised beneath cerebral translations of the Greek and Latin. A more faithful translation of this passage might be "set their hearts on" or "attune themselves to" the things of the Spirit.

In these passages in Matthew, First Corinthians, and Romans, we meet a distinction between styles of feeling. Ways of sensing that are worldly, childish, and fleshly are distinguished from ways of feeling that are godly, mature, and spiritual.

Senses Being Seasoned

We find ourselves gifted with a variety of powerful feelings and senses: delight, anger, affection, grief. And we come to see that none of these feelings is found in a pure or simple state. As the anthropologist Claude Lévi-Strauss has observed, human instincts are never "raw"; they are always "cooked"—shaped by one's culture and influenced by one's environment. The values and biases of family and neighborhood and society have, from the beginning of our days, been shaping our feelings and senses. Our ways of reacting—whether in rage or sorrow or affection—are never simply spontaneous. These are carefully, even if often unconsciously, learned from life around us. (If human feelings are never "raw," there are always those in the community whose feelings and senses are not only cooked but marinated, even pickled. Too thoroughly influenced by external forces, such persons have lost much of their spontaneity and liveliness.)

An image that may capture the proper maturing of our feelings and instincts is that of "seasoning." Growing up in a Christian family and participating in the life of a parish, we learn, gradually over many seasons, how Christians respond. We watch how those whom we cherish act. We learn their intuitive sense of how Christians treat their own bodies, how they are present to those whom they love. We observe how Christians feel about "others"—the poor, the sexually marginal, those who speak other languages and display different cultural habits. We learn over the years how Christians celebrate, the kind of events that bring this group together, how their minds and hearts and bodies are united in worship.

Christian maturing is the seasoning of instincts. In unconscious as well as conscious ways, our feelings are gradually formed by Christian values and hopes. Christian communities provide both the context and the examples for this formation of feelings. And, of course, as with every human and religious effort, we often fail at this formation. A family or parish may itself be less than Christian in some aspect of its own maturity-displaying an unholy distrust of the body or an outright rejection of some "others" who are mistakenly judged not to be of God's family. The young in such communities are shaped and seasoned in these unchristian ways. Their sensibilities are wounded or warped in ways inimical to Christian values. The challenge of Christian formation and education is to learn to provide the proper seasoning.

This metaphor of seasoning has within it a number of different elements. Obviously, it includes the notion of an external influence: the environment and atmosphere in which we grow up is shaping us. Second, seasoning suggests considerable duration: the shaping of our feelings and senses according to Christian hopes for justice and charity takes many seasons. Our sense of how to respond to different situations is formed over several decades by the values, stories, and convictions that are the milieu of our life. It is only gradually and with many reversals, failures, and confusions that we become seasoned Christians. To be seasoned also suggests being both "familiar with" and "good at." We have been at it sufficiently long enough to know, intuitively, how to respond; we know, now often without complex or arduous reflection, how we as Christians are to respond to this situation.

To be seasoned as a Christian is to have the values of Jesus Christ seep all the way through us. No longer an external authority or set of rules, they have been internalized and personalized. They have become us. To describe this transformation of our ways of feeling and sensing is to say that we have been "Christianized." Here the word does not refer to the event of our formal entrance into the Church; it refers to the inner shaping of our emotions and judgments.

This process of being seasoned must be ongoing in our lives, since we are never fully and finally matured. But the result of this process is that our instincts become trustworthy. Never infallible, our feelings nonetheless become, in time, reliable. The mature Christian is one whose sense—about when to express anger, about how to show affection, about who is my "neighbor"—can be trusted. Shaped and seasoned by Christian values, our intuition becomes dependable. Our feelings are transformed so that we experience them neither as alien nor as simply unpredictable. They become positive resources in our life, part of an inner authority whose movements we can trust. We mature in our faith life, then, as we learn to consult and trust the authority of our seasoned senses.

Another image to help us appreciate the process by which our feelings mature is that of tempering. This metaphor suggests a powerful substance, such as steel, that requires definite and careful shaping. Our emotions are also energies that await refining. The values and hopes handed on by followers of Jesus Christ act on our feelings and senses to temper them, to give them increased flexibility and strength. Our feelings, uncared for and untempered, are likely to become inflexible and brittle. We speak of a person being ill-tempered. Easy to anger, not especially sympathetic, such a person displays neither flexibility nor gracefulness. Tempering gives resilience to both blade and emotion. Untempered, both are more likely to break under pressure. Christian formation intends a special tempering of human feelings. The strength of this metaphor may lie in its reminder that our emotions are not to be suppressed or enslaved. They do, however, await a certain maturing, a development that will strengthen rather than weaken them. When our affections can consistently support and enliven our commitments, when our assertiveness encourages and guides our actions for justice, then we experience the strength of emotion that is well tempered.

Such is the special fruit of Christian adulthood. With these inner resources to rely on, we are less susceptible to the worldly forces that would seduce our feelings. Or, in Saint Paul's words, "We must no longer be children, tossed to and fro and blown about by every wind of doctrine, by people's trickery, by their craftiness in deceitful scheming" (Ephesians 4:14). Gradually seasoned by the values of Jesus Christ, we come into possession of trustworthy senses. While still failing and at times still fooling ourselves, we can more habitually and more thoroughly trust our responses and intuitions. Thus matured, we become ready for that most important exercise of Christian stewardship: handing on to the next generation the practical wisdom of how Christians feel and act and believe.

A Community's Sense of Faith

If as Christians we have been apprehensive about the role of the senses in personal maturing, we have been doubly doubtful about the place of feelings in community life. At one level we rightly fear the rule of feeling in a group: the memory of Hitler manipulating the emotions of the masses lingers in our historical memory. At another we are aware of the negative effects of conflict and cliques on a group's stability.

Feelings and emotions can become destructive in group life. But here, as in the life of the individual, we recognize that growth requires not the denial but the maturing of these powerful forces. There must be some parallel process by which a group of Christians, as a group, comes gradually to form and trust its shared feelings and instincts of faith. A group's maturing in the faith develops as it purifies and comes to trust its intuitions of how it is to act. This realization recalls a theological category with a long and varied history, "the sense of the faithful."

The roots of this notion lie in the conviction that the Spirit dwells within each genuine community of faith. This indwelling shapes the moods and influences the movements of a group of believers. This maturing "sense" of its faith supports and guides its decisions as a community. One practical exercise of this sense of faith in the earliest communities was their selection of leaders; such a judgment relied on intuitions about the kind and style of leadership they needed. Another exercise of the community's intuitive judgment would be seen in its decisions to send out missionaries, to set aside funds for the poor, to struggle to resolve internal conflicts. These decisions often met some resistance; but the group, seasoned by its memories of Jesus, sensed how it should act.

Just over a century ago, John Cardinal Newman turned to this notion of the sense of the faithful to explain how religious doctrine itself develops and expands. Newman argued that different Christian communities embrace, at a level of feeling or intuition, the deepest beliefs of Christianity. Newman defined this sense of the faithful "as a sort of instinct...deep in the bosom of the mystical body." Only over time does the official Church recognize and clarify these intuitions in formal teachings. Newman's argument was revolutionary in its insistence that a community is more than a docile recipient of Church teaching. This sense or instinct in a community is a source of its active expression of faith; it is the root of the group's maturity and generativity.

Another characteristic of the sense of the faithful according to Newman is its role in guarding against error. Mature communities defend against false teaching and unchristian attitudes. It is the maturity of its seasoned sense of faith that allows a community to "at once feel" that a certain decision or development is wrong. To expand Newman's image of a bodily instinct, the sense of the faithful allows this part of the body of Christ to sense foreign matter, to recognize the effects of harmful elements that may have gotten into the system. Such a seasoned instinct would recognize and reject both humanistic fads and fundamentalistic biases that attempt to pass as Christian insight.

In Vatican II we find a renewed enthusiasm for this sense of faith expected of Christian communities. The Council's document on the Church speaks of a "sense of the faith which characterizes the People as a whole," ensuring accord and fidelity in the faith (see Dogmatic Constitution on the Church). And this is more than a passive or simply docile sense. This intuition of belief has three functions:

It *clings* without fail to the faith once delivered to the saints (cf. Jude 3), *penetrates* it more deeply by accurate insights and *applies* it more thoroughly to life.

(# 12; OUR EMPHASIS)

If the first verb suggests stability and continuity, the second and third point to development and change. This instinct is the impetus for the deeper insight into our shared life of faith that arises as our different communities apply the faith "more thoroughly to life."

This renewed interest in a generative sense of faith abiding in the Christian community continued in the 1980 synod of Catholic bishops, which focused on Christian family life. Participants repeatedly referred to the Church's need to listen to the life experience of mature women and men in Christian families in order to learn about the changing face of marriage. The sense of the faithful about Christian marriage in today's world will be revealed in communities of married believers. The fourth resolution of the synod observed that this sense of the faithful "flows from those Christian families in which the sacrament of marriage is realized and revealed as an experience of faith."

The institutional Church continues to become more appreciative of what it must learn from the lived faith of mature believers. This appreciation is leading us beyond more rhetorical and pious uses of the phrase "sense of the faithful." We are beginning to acknowledge that such a sense, maturing with different rhythms in different societies and communities, must necessarily be plural and divergent. The ideals of universal agreement and conformity must be complemented by a tolerance for difference and even conflict. Dissent, debate, and divergence in faith—obvious and necessary aspects of the Church from its inception—are yet to be fully accepted as parts of this sense of the faithful.

Ministering to a Community's Sense of Faith

A ministry to a community's sense of faith begins in the expectation that this group has such a sense. The maturing of a Christian community includes the development of a trustworthy instinct of what its faith is and how, practically, it is to be lived. Such a sense of faith, as more than rhetorical, will express the individuality of this community as well as its oneness with the universal Church; it will expectably bring this community both into a deeper unity and a livelier tension with the whole Church. Such a particularized sense of faith will also ground a community's identity and vocation.

It helps the community come into a more profound sense of what it is for. Out of this sense of faith is born a community's generative ministry. Recognizing who we are and what our faith is for, we come to sense how we are to act. Our ministry—how we in this group of believers are to care for and challenge the world around us in the name of Jesus Christ—takes its shape and direction from our practical sense of faith.

If the ministry to a community's sense of faith begins in the expectation that it have such a personalized awareness, this ministry proceeds as it forms and clarifies this sense of faith. Since it is a kind of collective conscience, this sense of faith always requires formation. The values of Jesus Christ and the gospels are brought again and again into this community's life— in its liturgies, its educational efforts, its practical decisions about money and other resources—and allowed to shape its actions.

As the sense of faith of our communities matures over many years, it will need repeated clarification. Using the language of the Constitution on the Church, we will have to examine how this community is living out its faith: "clinging" to the faith of its tradition; "penetrating" this faith more deeply and accurately; and "applying" it more thoroughly to the changes in contemporary life.

This continual clarification will also teach a faith community about its role in the larger Church. As the community reflects on its own faith, it clarifies how it is in accord with and in tension with the larger Church. Thus a community may, for example, come to certain convictions about justice that put it in conflict with the official Church position on the use of diocesan funds. As this community examines these convictions, aware that its own insights are always in need of purification, it may also present these convictions as challenges to the diocese and other leadership groups in the Church. When communities can do this maturely—that is, with concreteness and patience and without personal attack or ultimatum—they perform a most important part of their own ministry. Such a ministry, that of a local community of faith to the larger Church, depends on a community's trust in its sense of faith. As with the individual conscience of a Christian, this collective conscience must not only be formed and purified but also trusted. Maturity, for a community as well as for an individual, includes the ability to follow trustworthy instincts of faith.

A mature community will be able to withstand rejection: its tested sense of identity and vocation can survive conflict and disagreement. It is aware that new insights generated by particular communities will often be rejected by leadership groups in the Church—sometimes because they are wrong, sometimes because they are new.

The life of the extrarational—our feelings, emotions, intuitions—has long disquieted Christians. We are gradually becoming more comfortable with the role of these powerful parts of ourselves in our growth in holiness: seasoned senses, become reliable guides, lead us toward prudent and wise judgments. We are only beginning to imagine how this same dynamic directs the religious maturing of a group. A community's affections and angers and dreads can be healed and tempered over time by the values of Jesus Christ. This is, in practice, the development of a community's sense of faith. On these fragile but maturing instincts, the future of our shared life depends.

Reflective Exercise

Recall an important decision in your recent past with which you were pleased.

1. Call to memory the reflections, discussions, and hesitations that surrounded that choice.
2. How did you come to a "sense" of what decision to make?

Then reflect on your intuitions about expressing affection for others.

1. How has this sense changed and matured over the past decade?
2. In what ways have you grown more comfortable and confident in your own style of emotional expression?
3. How has this style been seasoned and purified in recent years?

CHAPTER SIX

The Virtue of Self-Intimacy

A reflection on the virtue of self-intimacy begins with the realization that we are, each one of us, plural. Each of us is an amalgam of different and even conflicting hopes and fears. We combine within ourselves a variety of ambitions and ideals; there are so many things we would like to be and to do. Accompanying the ambitions and dreams within us are our apprehensions and doubts. Some of these are momentary or occur only in certain situations; others, we find, endure. They accompany us throughout the years of our life.

This pluralism we find within us may remain a scandal and a secret. We have learned that only "crazy people" have conflicting, ambivalent, unresolved elements inside. "Normal people"—most of those we see around us—appear so stable and balanced. My own interior life, with its abrupt surprises, its anxieties and unfinishedness, is embarrassing. Perhaps it is to be suffered, but hardly to be explored or shared—even with myself. Self-intimacy is a virtue by which I grow in awareness and acceptance of this particular human being I am becoming.

It adds to the strength of identity, my sense of clarity and confidence about who I am, a tolerance and affection for this specific person. It is a strength of mature self-love which is the ground for my love of and care for others.

The less we need to keep our plural self a secret, the more alert we are to a crucial task of psychological development and Christian maturing. This is the task of attending to the ongoing revelation of a self that is becoming. Our richly complex selves, created by and inhabited by our God, reveal themselves only over time and only to the careful observer. The self-revelation of God which takes place in nature and in other people, our lovers and enemies alike, also occurs within us. The presence and self-revelation of God in our own particular lives lead us beyond narcissism and invite us to religious introspection.

There are two complementary challenges to psychological and religious development in adult life, and in their balance appears maturity. The first has received more attention in the Christian tradition: the challenge to change, to reform, to be converted. We know ourselves to be sinners, selfish, destructive, and untrusting. In our Christian life we are challenged to change, to respond to God's efforts to transform and heal this wounded self. This is the call to *metanoia*—Christian conversion and change of heart. This requires much effort and a kind of "holy intolerance" with who we are. It is important to note the appropriateness of this intolerance, especially at the beginning of adult life. Young adults are often intolerant of others and of themselves as well. Similarly, in the early stages of their new conviction, converts of many kinds are notoriously intolerant of those who do not share their own clear vision. As we saw in chapter three, this impatience with imperfection often characterizes the disciple as well.

Yet there comes a period of maturing when such intolerance becomes less "holy." Then is glimpsed the other aspect of *metanoia*: the challenge to be converted to a deeper love and acceptance of ourselves. As we continue to change—to become more virtuous and less selfish, less destructive and untrusting—we are also challenged to come to a more tolerant love of this particular amalgam of strengths and weaknesses that we find ourselves to be. This challenge is essentially an invitation to greater self-intimacy.

The movement of self-intimacy and greater self-love is not a settling into smugness or complacency. It is a call to bring about a deeper harmony and integration of the variety of things that I am. It is an invitation to move beyond the useful self-denial of an earlier stage in life when it was perhaps necessary for me to look away from some ambiguous, humiliating, or confusing parts of myself. As we mature, we seem to be asked—and for Christians this is a religious request—to befriend ourselves. We are invited to a new level of comfort with our own particular and peculiar self and to a more appreciative familiarity with what God is doing with us and despite us.

Befriending Myself
As Plural Now

We are, each of us, plural not only over time, through the history of what we have done and who we have been; we are plural now. This very day I find myself multiple, with enthusiasm for many parts of my life and apprehension about many others. I am, often at once, courageous and afraid, hopeful and despondent. I find my best efforts of care for others are laced with a variety of motives, accompanied by a range of diverse feelings. And I realize as I mature that this variety of motives and feelings does not necessarily make me bad, but it does make me who I am. This particular combination of abilities and limits, of creativity and stubbornness, is who I am. The challenge of self-intimacy is to better understand this plural self and to better love it.

There is much information available to us about who we are and how we are doing. At times this information takes dramatic form, in an ulcer or heart attack. Exhaustion and depression may likewise signal an imbalance, a lack of harmony or integration in our life. Psychological and religious maturity entails the ability to attend to both the dramatic and everyday information available to us. A different kind of discipline, influenced by cultural norms of achievement and self-sufficiency, urges us to push ahead, to keep going and ignore this information. Such a discipline is a form of self-denial in a quite unchristian sense. Its fruit is more often an exhausted and angry "achiever" than a generous and concerned adult.

Self-intimacy begins in attending to the information from within. As we listen, we learn more about both our limits and our best hopes. I can begin to set aside the expectations that others have of me and my own idealistic but abstract goals, replacing these with a clearer and more concrete awareness of what my own life offers. I come into the rhythm of my adulthood and into a greater comfort and patience with my own life journey.

Self-intimacy can result in a clearer sense of my motives. More aware of why I overwork or get angry or depressed, I have a better opportunity to heal these parts of myself—whether this healing entails overcoming or becoming comfortable with them.

The goal of this task of befriending a plural self is "self-possession." Each of us probably knows a few people who are deeply comfortable with who they are. Neither resigned nor overachievers, they are doing well what they can, quietly aware of their own limits and needs. Such people are at ease with themselves. They have found their rhythm; they have, in the deepest sense, come into their vocation. And perhaps best of all, they like themselves.

I may even sense some of this movement in myself. I find, for example, that I can only work *this* hard. I wish I were stronger and could work as long as some others around me, but I cannot—and that is acceptable to me. I acknowledge that this is how I look—not taller, not more attractive or youthful, not with more commanding presence. I look like this—and it is acceptable, too. Actually, it is better than acceptable; this is who I am and I like it. There are, as well, certain recurring fears and doubts that seem to be me. I once assumed that effort and the years would rid me of them. Now it looks as though they are with me "for the duration." So I will make the best of them. I may even come to embrace these inner demons, these once-intolerable weaknesses. Saint Paul may have had something like this in mind with his reference to the thorn in his flesh. Certain weaknesses and peculiarities we cannot shake; they are us. Even God seems content not to remove them. Self-intimacy invites us to be more tolerant of even these aspects of who we are.

Finally, self-intimacy allows us to live in the present. Self-acceptance means liking myself *now*, at this age in my life. With growth in this virtue, I am rescued from a cultural obsession with youth, an obsession which would have me apologize for my present age as I grow older. I am more able to be present to every year of my life. I need not deny or hide my age—because I like who I am now.

The religious insight that supports this call to self-acceptance and love is that we cannot wait until we are perfect to love ourselves. A myth of perfection has injured much Christian effort at religious growth. In the pursuit of perfection, we have been allowed to hate ourselves as sinners, imperfect, flawed. When we are surprised by human love, we may think that we are loved only because the other person does not really know us. We are tempted to hide our flaws, pretend to be someone else in order to hold on to this undeserved love. But if we are lucky we learn that our friend really loves *us*—all of who we are, flaws and all. It may take this lesson to remind us that God loves us as we are. In God's sight we are lovely now; it is not our good works, our achievements, or even our penitence that renders us magically lovely. It is in being loved, to paraphrase Chesterton, that we become lovely. This is true for self-intimacy: I am invited to love myself, not in the light of future improvement, but now as I am. More comfortable with both my particularity and my loveliness, I become better at loving others.

Reconciling Myself As Plural Over Time

As the journey of our life proceeds we accumulate a history: we have been many places, lived many roles. The pluralism of this historical self is rarely one of radical or total change. We recognize a continuity in ourselves from child to adolescent to adult. Enduring memories and hopes bind the journey and identify it, in all its stages, as *mine*. We may meet people who represent extremes of personal change or stability. There are some who cut off their roots, trying to disengage themselves from a hated or intolerable past; they may even change their names in a search for a different identity. At the other extreme we meet people who have refused change, who have held rigidly to what they have always been. But most of us live between these extremes. As we continue to change in response to life's demands and invitations, we find ourselves unfolding, we discover unsuspected interests and unanticipated abilities. And we learn the deception of language. A single word—such as *priest* or *wife* or *worker*—has been used to describe me for the past fifteen or thirty years. Yet I find I have played a multitude of roles under that single category; I have understood myself very differently at different points over those years.

My present self, then, is an accumulation of what I have been and what I have done—successes and failures, promises kept and commitments left behind. This personal history abides in me in various states of consciousness and harmony. By midlife, however, I can expect this history to demand some of my attention. About this time many adults find themselves invited to reexamine this history and to integrate certain aspects of it into their lives more explicitly.

This invitation to a reassessment of my life may arise in a sudden confrontation with a tender part of my past. I am suddenly reminded of the way my parent—or teacher, or superior, or spouse—has treated me. I am surprised by the anger this recollection generates. Blame joins anger: these people hurt me and are to blame for my troubles now. In this anger there is revealed to me an important part of my past, of myself, that has remained unforgiven. I see a part of my life that is ugly and painful, an unforgiven part of myself that I had kept hidden but now demands attention. Or the sore, unforgiven part of my past may be something that I did to myself. Some mistake or poor choice now reappears; guilt and regret flow again within me. The revelation is the same: this is a part of myself that I have hated or denied or been ashamed of. Now I am invited to be reconciled with it.

There seem to be three options when such uncomfortable information begins to surface in us. We can get busy and try to bury this disturbance from the past. Here the hope is to ignore it. We treat it as a distraction; we repress it (again) and hope it will go away. A second option is to seize, with renewed vigor, the feelings of blame or guilt and give ourselves over to the process of punishment—of my parents, or spouse, or myself. This option is to respond to the distress without discerning its opportunity. A third option is to confront the blame or the guilt as an important initial phase of this interior invitation. As we experience these strong feelings about our past, we may eventually experience as well the invitation to forgive. This powerful, negative event really happened and did, in fact, influence my life. But, as I may find, I no longer need to blame my parents or other authorities; I no longer need to carry this guilt about my own behavior in the past. This sore and wounded part of my past—part of myself—I can forgive. I can embrace this part of myself, welcoming it into my present life. This is not an embrace that magically transforms the past; it does not make either the pain or the scar disappear. But this embrace and reconciliation with my past is a kind of exorcism: this part of myself, with its harbored rage and guilt, loses its power over me. As I come, over some time, to forgive this event of my past, I dissolve its destructive power in my life. I no longer have to deny or avoid this part of me. It cannot hurt me as it used to because I have embraced it, welcomed it home, and in so doing relieved it of its power.

How is such an extraordinary thing possible? Christians have learned of this in the life of Jesus Christ. The possibility of forgiveness is one of the most startling of Christian revelations. When our hearts harden (even against ourselves) and forgiveness seems impossible or intolerable, the Gospel tells us otherwise. Christian revelation tells us we can expect the extraordinary even from ourselves. And it also proclaims the effect of this powerful act of forgiving: the past can be changed. The notion of fate suggests that what is done is done. Forgiveness contradicts this: it gives us power to change the past and the force of its failures. We can forgive what has been done to us—by parents, by the Church, by our spouse, even by ourselves. The past, our personal past, is not as finished as we have been led to believe. It is alive and well, or alive and ailing, in our memories and recollections. At different junctures in life, we are invited to explore this lively part of ourselves and to further the continual process of reconciliation and integration that describes our growth in the virtue of self-intimacy.

The reconciliation with a wounded, unforgiven part of our past exorcises its power over us. This important result of reconciliation can be discussed in terms of self-defense and the conservation of energy. Self-defense is not, simply, bad. We all need defenses to survive the demands and assaults of life. Yet we often sense that our tendency is to overdefend. As we catch ourselves repeatedly checking our makeup, or straightening our tie, or smoothing our hair, we can recognize the energy that we expend, daily, in guarding this fragile self. With humor, or curtness, or credentials, we armor ourself against anticipated assaults, real and imaginary.

As we mature and come to a greater comfort with who we are, we need to expend less energy on defense. More comfortable with this particular person that I am, with my many limits and strengths, I have less need to defend or prove myself before others. Having learned about my loveliness, foibles and all, from loved ones and from God, I need give less attention and energy to hiding my weaknesses, to showing my best profile and disguising my flaws, physical or spiritual.

This is energy saved, energy conserved and redeemed. Rescuing this energy from the purposes of self-defense, we can invest it in efforts of care and love of others. My partner, my children, my career—all of these consume my energy. Self-intimacy invites us to a more efficient and virtuous use of this personal power. And this is an ironic sign of its genuineness: by careful, loving attention to our own life we liberate the personal energy formerly given to defense and repression, freeing it for more powerful care for the world beyond ourselves.

Narcissus and Religious Insight

Christians have learned to be squeamish about "looking inside." Such introspection is often felt to be selfish, distracting us from other persons and from our God whom we should serve. Christian distrust of self is rooted in a theology of the Fall, which interprets original sin as a turning in on the self. This theology understands human nature as inclined toward narrow self-absorption; it urges us to learn to avert our gaze. Christian asceticism, in such an understanding, turns our vision away from ourselves—from our bodies, to be sure, but also from our own ambitions and hopes. All are most likely to be selfish. If we are corrupted on the inside, then introspection serves no good religious purpose. Rather it moves toward narcissism. Self-intimacy here is not a virtue but a vice, a form of spiritual self-abuse.

About such introspection, two questions are especially relevant: how we inspect ourselves and what we expect to see. Narcissus gazed into a pond and saw himself, or thought he did. This watery, insubstantial reflection fascinated him, absorbing his attention. He looked again and again, distracted from other activities.

This same image of gazing into the pond of oneself appears often in the Buddhist religious tradition, but with quite a different meaning. Each person, according to one Buddhist tradition, is like a pond of murky, agitated water. We are called to quiet this turbulence, to discipline our lives until the murkiness settles and the water is clear and still. Then a disciplined look into the water reveals not the individual's image but that of the Buddha nature. Hidden in the depths is not just my private reflection, but an identity that unites me to all other living things and, by so doing, tells me who I am. Such introspection leads not to a distracted absorption in myself, but to a recognition of who I am and where I belong. Christian introspection, itself undertaken to calm the turbulence that our fears, ambitions, and distractions cause in our life, reveals both our identity and God's presence. My profoundest identity is not my individualistic, isolated self. This identity is—and here Buddhist and Christian mystics would agree—a common identity, a oneness with others in God (or in Buddha). This is a parable and an irony: it is by a disciplined introspection that we can find our community with others. To look within apart from such faith is to come face to face with only myself; to look within with faith is to come face to face with God. In this recognition, this "enlightenment," sudden or gradual, we are rescued from narcissism because we see both who we are and to whom we belong.

So there are different ways to look within. Narcissism, as a compulsion and a distraction, has me searching repeatedly and desperately for a self. Such a search is not a sign of self-intimacy but proof of its absence. Narcissism is not self-love, but an inability to love and to be comfortable with myself. The compulsiveness of narcissistic persons, who must search for "who I am" again and again in the mirror of every new performance and relationship, reminds us of their discomfort with the self. Their busy search signals a disease with the self. Narcissistic introspection arises not from self-esteem but from its opposite.

Christian introspection is guided by a conviction of an inner loveliness and an enduring presence. We may not always experience this presence or our own loveliness, but we believe in it. We look within in response to the invitation to befriend this person so beloved of God. Self-intimacy as a Christian virtue develops over many years of patient, tolerant listening to this plural and unfolding self. I come gradually to better distinguish personal limitations that must be changed from those that must be tolerated and embraced. As I come into a more penetrating awareness of myself, I see not only my limits and incompleteness but my loveliness as well. Perhaps I may even come to a tangible sense of a presence within, a presence that does not distract me from my own identity, but encourages me further into it.

Midlife and Mutuality: Where Self-Intimacy Grows

Knowledge takes time; the self-knowledge that issues in a deeper respect and tolerance for the particular person I am takes decades.

In the early years of adult life, we have as yet only a modest amount of information about ourselves. Possibilities are many; opportunities, ideals, and dreams of success abound. Others' expectations still tightly wrap our own hopes. Our energy both excites and distracts us. In young adulthood we necessarily spend much time checking external criteria of how we are doing; we look for ways to "prove ourselves," to have someone or something testify to our identity and worth.

Maturing describes the process of "finding ourselves"— coming to awareness of how competent we are at what we do and how limited. This awareness is less and less founded on external criteria or others' approval. As we find ourselves we realize there is less need to prove ourselves.

What was unavailable to us at twenty-five becomes clearer by forty-five or so: an awareness of strengths we did not earlier suspect; the presence of dreams that previously lay buried under the "shoulds" of others' expectations; the concrete shape of fears only hinted at in our youth. All this suggests that self-intimacy is a virtue that has its special season in midlife.

Self-intimacy is not a private enterprise. Few of us find it effective to retreat to isolation in order to learn about and come to love ourselves. For most of us, community and family are the arenas for this challenge. It is colleagues and coworkers, spouses and children, friends and sometimes even enemies who reflect back to us information about who we are and what we are becoming. We learn that our intimates frequently see parts of us before we do; this is both an exciting and a humiliating aspect of being "up close," whether in work or in love. My partner is thus a vehicle of this self-revelation. This unmasking of myself, performed by those closest to me, reveals me more surely to myself and invites me to a new self-acceptance.

As a virtue, self-intimacy depends on skills for its practical development. Sensing the disturbances or dreams within, we are challenged to take the time to listen; as we listen we need the ability to name our feelings. Courage and skill are required if we are to share this confusing or exciting information with those closest to us. Such skillful listening, naming, and sharing guide the processes of reconciliation and forgiveness that are such an important part of self-intimacy at midlife.

Loneliness and Solitude

We all spend much time alone. However busy we become, we still live "in ourselves," having to contend always with our inner life. Loneliness and solitude describe two very different ways we are with ourselves; each is related to our maturing in self-intimacy.

Loneliness has many connotations. Here we would have this word describe the experience of not being at home with myself. I can be lonely in a crowd as well as when alone. Loneliness occurs when I am alienated from my own resources. Distrustful, or frightened, or disgusted by who I am, I cannot be at home with myself. I am uncomfortable with what is inside and need to distract myself; I turn up the music, talk louder, get busy. When we are lonely we find difficulty with recollection or prayer; our aloneness distracts us from ourselves.

Madonna Kolbenschlag discusses envy as characteristic of persons who are not at home with themselves. Lacking confidence in myself, I need to be on the watch for others who may be doing better, looking lovelier, getting ahead. With no trust in the inner criteria of my worth, I am forced to look outside for indications of my identity and value. This gives a new and sadder meaning to the phrase "looking out for myself." Living in such an other-directed fashion, I am prey not only to envy but also depression. Depression is a serious malaise, a discomfort with who I am. I am dissatisfied with my limits, my shortcomings, my own particularity. Depressed and envious persons wish they were someone else and somewhere else. They are not at home with themselves. Kolbenschlag suggests that envy may be a particular temptation for women.

In classic Christian theology, the deadliest sin is pride and self-assertion. Envy, on the other hand, is the sin of those who fail to assert themselves, who fail to find and to become themselves. The Christian virtue which strengthens us to overcome the sin of envy, as well as the curse of depression and loneliness, is self-intimacy.

Solitude is another experience of being by myself. Its connotations are different than those of loneliness: solitude suggests not an alienation but a mellow quiet—a comfort, perhaps mixed with sadness, in being alone. Another translation of solitude might be "being at home with myself." We began this reflection with the image of ourselves as plural, comprising a variety of abilities, shortcomings, and ambiguities. The home of the self, then, is peopled with many residents. Self-intimacy and solitude suggest a certain domestic tranquillity. The mellowness of solitude reminds us that presence to myself is not always an experience of delight. Self-intimacy entails not a banishment or denial of every failed or incomplete part of myself, but an embracing of these aspects. Solitude suggests a deep peacefulness with this particular person that I am. To return to the metaphor of the self as a home, every house is, in part, haunted. We speak of families having skeletons in the closet. So with my own interior abode. The lonely person, uncomfortable with many inhabitants of the self, tends to stay away from home. In solitude, I become more aware of, and at ease with, the skeletons and unexorcised ghosts of my inner life. This ease contributes, in turn, to a befriending and taming—the integration of my plural self.

The fruit of self-intimacy, experienced in solitude, is the ability to be alone. I do not need to clutter my life with activity and busywork. I can, at times, stop talking and let the noise settle. This is possible because I know that what I will be left with—just myself—is good. There will be not just agitation and guilt and disappointment to contend with, there will also be gentle humor (how strange I am!) and thankfulness (how blessed my life has been!). In periods of solitude—whether enforced, as with illness, or chosen, as in prayer and days of retreat—I can listen more trustingly to the inner voices. And among these many contending sounds I may hear the voice of God blessing me with new dreams and ambitions.

Reflective Exercise

To grasp more concretely the multiplicity of your own sense of self, it may be useful to turn to a chart or picture. Start by drawing a large circle on a sheet of paper. Within the circle, record some of the roles you fill in your family and job and elsewhere. Place close to the center of the circle those roles that are most significant to you; place others at a distance that shows their lesser importance to you.

Then add within the circle the names of three or four things that you do really well or aspects of yourself that you especially like. Finally, place in the circle three or four personal limitations that you know and have come to accept.

Spend some time savoring this picture of yourself. Note which roles you place closest to the center and which are farther away. Note what you chose to add concerning your strengths and limitations. What does this representation of yourself say to you now?

Now list outside the circle those aspects of yourself with which you are most uncomfortable. Consider each in turn: Is it a fault or failing that needs to be overcome? Or is it a genuine part of yourself that needs to be befriended, that asks to be welcomed into the larger circle? Is it, perhaps, even an unadmitted strength?

Reflect on how you might deal with each of these unwanted aspects in ways that contribute to the harmony of your plural self.

CHAPTER SEVEN

Re-Imagining
Personal Power

"Stir up your power, O Lord, and come." In this Advent prayer we invoke God's power and invite it into our lives. As we mature our own power is stirred; both virtue and confidence grow strong. But if it is obvious that Christian maturing is about power, it is also unnerving. We have been schooled in a reluctance about power. We experience power interiorly in surges of anger and sexual arousal. If these forces are healthy, they are also frequently frightening. Our social imaginations are wounded by the devastating shape that power has taken in public: the overshadowing cloud of Hiroshima; the scent of Auschwitz; the sights of Vietnam. Power seems demonic, so often destructive.

Lord Acton's judgment comes quickly to mind: "Power tends to corrupt, and absolute power corrupts absolutely." If this is so, then becoming holy must mean avoiding power and its corruptions. But even as we cling to safer ideals of meekness and humility of heart, we sense we have succumbed to a narrow view of power. Can power be rescued from this solely negative interpretation? Power is destructive—and creative. Power is demonic—and holy. Can this rich ambiguity be recovered and celebrated as a part of Christian life? In the following pages we will explore the experience of power in adult life for clues to its shape as a Christian virtue.

The word *virtue* means, simply, power. We must remember that Yahweh answered to the name of Power in the Hebrew Scriptures. A more imaginative look at the New Testament suggests that this is a story about power: God's power, become tangible in Jesus Christ, seeks to season our lives in various gifts and virtues. And Lord Acton's statement finds its complement in the gospel accounts of Jesus: power tends to heal, and absolute power heals absolutely. Jesus' words give hope and his touch heals. By his life he announces a power that knows no limit to its healing. If we can imagine power as more than corrupting, we can begin to explore its role in Christian maturing. In this exploration we may come to recognize the shape of personal power in our own lives, as our real but limited strengths grow into reliable virtues.

Power is about strength. And strength comes in various shapes in the different contexts of our lives. Among teenagers, for example, the most important sign of strength may be athletic ability or good looks. In a suburban neighborhood, it may be the prestige of my occupation or the size of my paycheck. And the world community watches with concern as nations vie for superiority in the destructive strengths of war.

Discussions of power are complicated and often confusing. Two clarifications can assist our effort to understand the place of power in our lives. First, it is misleading to treat power as a thing, as though it were an internal "packet" of energy. Power is not an "entity" but a way of interacting. Power is more a process than a thing. Power points to something that happens between people, something going on, an interaction. Power is not so much a possession as a way of relating.

Second, it is useful to distinguish between personal power and social power. Personal power points to my awareness of myself as strong, the ways I find myself capable or coercive in interaction with others. Social power refers to the broader experiences of strength among us—the energy in this group, the authority of this organization. Social power also involves an awareness of the differences in strength among us—what these differences are and how we will deal with them. We do not all possess equally the kinds of strength that are seen as important in this group, whether that be intelligence or goodness or money or political clout. The patterns of social power in any group reflect the ways that members recognize and negotiate these differences in strength.

Social power and personal power are closely related. It is in a group—in the family or on a work team or as a member of a civic organization—that most of us become aware of our own power. The definitions of power in these groups (social power) influence my awareness of how I am strong (personal power). The group's sense of the strengths that are worthwhile often becomes the criterion I use to judge whether I am powerful. The influence can also go in the other direction. When there are changes in an awareness of personal power, the patterns of social authority and group leadership shift as well. We have examples of this in the current experience of the Church, as laypersons look for new patterns of dialogue and accountability in their relationship with the clergy. Acknowledging these connections between personal and social power, we focus our discussion here on personal power.

The Faces of Personal Power

Power, we have suggested, is not a possession but a social transaction. It is one of the ways in which we come face to face as adults. Care, conflict, and control: each is an experience of power through which we touch one another and influence one another's lives. This interaction of personal power wears at least five faces.

Faces of Personal Power

Mode	Experienced As	Needed In
Power On	initiative and influence	adult competence
Power Over	coordination and control	organizational leadership
Power Against	competition and conflict	assertion and negotiation
Power For	service and nurturance	parenthood and ministry
Power With	mutuality and collaboration	interdependence and dependability

Power On

We see the first face of power in our acts of initiation and influence: "Things happen because of me." It may be a very simple act: I find I can make another person smile. It may be a more complex exercise of influence: I present a new plan at work, and it receives serious consideration. Or in a troubled friendship, I risk a confrontation that moves our relationship to a deeper level.

"Power on" is the simplest, most innocent face of power. I find I can do things, my actions make a difference. I am more than a child or a passive victim. I can influence my world—at least in some ways. This first experience of power does not yet confront the difference between care and constraint or feel the tension between influence and coercion.

But even this simplest form of power is not always easy to attain. A variety of factors can defeat this personal strength. A dominating parent may so manage my life that I am left with no sense of autonomous power: I am cared for, but I cannot shape my own world. Or poverty may educate me in impotence: I am too weak, too ineffectual to influence others. I am encouraged to see myself as a victim, unable to be powerful except, perhaps, in self-destructive acts of violence.

Through the experience of "power on" I come to sense that I am an agent in my own life and that I have resources which enable me to influence my environment. My strength is not simply "housed" within me, it moves beyond me to influence people and events. I am strong enough to have an impact.

"Power on" gives me a basic sense of my own autonomy and adequacy. It leads to an appreciation of my special competence: I do some things well. This sense of effectiveness gives me confidence to take on the responsibilities of adult life, both in love and work. Having a skill, mastering a difficult task, being able to bring a project to completion—each of these can bring with it a perception of myself as strong, as having resources that can be counted on to see me through.

Paradoxically, such mature autonomy is a foundation of adult intimacy as well. Marriage and family counselors know how much the conviction "I can make it on my own if I have to" is part of mature interdependent love. This strength of autonomy is not all that is involved; to grow in intimacy I must also be able to take the risk of not going it alone, of counting on you to be with me. But if I cannot trust my own resources I am likely to become too dependent, insisting that you satisfy my needs because I do not feel adequate in myself.

Power Over

A second face of adult strength appears as we are challenged not just to influence others but to take charge. Many of the responsibilities of daily life require this kind of power. Serving on the parish council, disciplining our teenage children, supervising a production team, even returning a defective piece of merchandise—each of these is difficult for me if I have no sense of "power over," of the possibility and legitimacy of my giving direction to other people.

But "power over" often appears as a frowning face of power because it seems to suggest force and manipulation. Perhaps it is the word *over* that frightens us, conjuring up memories of bullies and bosses who used their power to dominate. For many of us, then, there are old wounds to be healed before we can move comfortably into the realm of leading others.

The earlier expression of power was in my own strength; I can do something. This second face of power introduces me to managing the power of others. To assume leadership in a group, I must be able to generate and focus energies that go beyond my own. Caring for a family, too, requires the coordination and control of diverse and often conflicting energies. In any role of supervision—as foreman, as teacher, as mentor—I must be able to exercise "power over." Without this kind of power among us, much of group life seems ineffective. Decisions are not carried out, resources are wasted, energies dissipate.

Most of us recognize the importance of this face of personal power, but we remain uneasy with it. Our ambivalence about "power over" may lie in the very different images and feelings that surround its two functions of coordination and control.

The word *coordination* may call up images of a dance troupe. We are impressed and delighted by the coordination of each dancer's movements in the precision of the company's performance. In "coordination" we see the harmony of disparate powers unified in a graceful effort.

But "control" evokes more sinister images: arms that hold us too tightly, rules that restrict our freedom. It may help to recall that the seemingly effortless coordination of the athlete comes only with exceptional control. The dancer's grace comes only in a body that has been well controlled, exercised again and again in disciplined movement. This tedious repetition and control are concealed in the final artistic product but are the sure supports of the performance.

But control remains a suspect exercise of power, and with good reason. In our recent social memory, control has so often been exercised in constraint and coercion. Leadership positions have often been used to pursue private gain rather than the common good. In these instances, "power over" loses its necessary nuances of shared goals and mutual accountability. It comes to be a mask for manipulation.

If we know that control can lead to coercion, we must acknowledge that the two are not simply synonyms. Definitions of control include "bringing together a number of resources"; "keeping a complicated effort on track"; "giving a sense of direction to a larger effort." These activities of control are essential in our life together. Without this kind of power among us, it is difficult for us to celebrate our sense of cohesion as a family or to chart our future as a religious congregation.

To remind ourselves that the exercise of control is not always manipulative, we might recall the power of the conductor in an orchestra or the director in a play. Each role requires "power over": the ability to focus a group's energies, to channel diverse resources into an organic whole. For the group to be successful here, the leader must have control. But the leader's control exists in context. Both the conductor and the musicians are accountable to the musical score. The goal of the joint effort lies outside of the leader's control; it provides the criterion by which the leader's control can be judged. Both the group and the leader are accountable to something beyond their ultimate control. When "power over" is exercised in this way, in pursuit of a common goal and in the context of mutual accountability, it can resist the temptation toward manipulation.

Our ambivalence about control helps explain some of the tensions today over the function of leadership in the community of faith. Ministry often includes roles of organizational management and institutional leadership. Increasingly we see a reluctance among ministers to move into these roles. This kind of leadership can seem a thankless task. It demands skills of initiation and restraint, empowerment and accountability. Yet the very exercise of these resources of "power over" seems tainted. Both the leader and the group are keenly sensitive about attitudes and actions that give hint of control. Most leaders realize that their success depends to a large degree on the support of group members, both reinforcing their right to lead and cooperating in the decisions made. This support can be seriously compromised when every exercise of control is likely to be interpreted as coercion. In the face of such suspicion, some leaders back away from the exercise of "power over." But without the freedom to exert "power over" when it is necessary, the burdens of organizational responsibility become overwhelming, even for talented and generous leaders. There are other talented people today who, knowing that a leadership position deprived of the resources of coordination and control is doomed to failure, refuse to take on this organizational role. In both instances, ministry suffers.

It is with good reason that we have been suspicious of organizational power. Yet there are signs in the Church today that we are moving beyond this widespread suspicion of our leaders. Slowly, in our dioceses and parishes and religious houses, we are coming to realize that without coordination and control our corporate effort is weakened. Little by little we are improving at distinguishing control from coercion: when leadership's control remains accountable to the common good, a good that is not interpreted solely by the leader, "power over" can be a graceful exercise of strength. Maturity requires not an abandonment of our suspicions of control but their clarification. We need to be able to welcome back among us the strengths of "power over." This strength, like any other, requires accountability and ongoing purification. But without it we are weaker, both personally and communally.

Power Against

A third mode of power, equally troublesome for many of us, takes its stance "against." This is power in its combative face. I experience my strength challenged by the people in my life or by the circumstances and obstacles I encounter. The awareness here includes an experience of struggle and opposition, even antagonism. At issue is whether I will be found adequate to the test, whether—in the face of some outside forces—my own strength will prevail.

This experience of power is a part of competitive games, where I match my strength and skill against that of an opponent. Winning, having my power prevail "against" my opponent, is important to me here. But as I learn to play well, I come to recognize that winning is not the only benefit involved in the game. There is the exhilaration of the contest itself, the opportunity to try my strength and further develop my skill. There is even the mellow lesson that I can lose without being humiliated and that I can fall without being shamed. Often the camaraderie of playing against one another is the chief benefit of the game, offering its own kind of companionship and intimacy.

To be sure, the game can degenerate into a struggle to win at whatever price, but it need not do so. And when a game does become such a battle we often sense that energies have gone awry and that something important in the contest itself has been lost.

To be able to contest, then, is a part of adult maturity. It is a resource of adult power important not only in competitive sports but even more so in the movements of competition, confrontation, and conflict that are part of the exercise of adult responsibility.

Increasingly we are aware, from both the findings of psychological research and the evidence of our own lives, of the place of competition and conflict in "up close" relationships. Conflict between spouses, struggles between parents and their teenage children, antagonism among different groups in the parish—these are normal and expectable dynamics of living with others. These conflicts can escalate toward hostility and hatred: this is part of our fear of power used "against." But conflict is not inevitably destructive. This powerful part of life "up close" can be harnessed in a way that turns its energy to good use, redistributing power among us, revitalizing our commitment to one another, suggesting fresh alternatives for the future.

To deal maturely with these dynamics of competition and conflict I must be somewhat comfortable with the experience of myself as powerful "against." I must know that I am strong enough to stand in the face of another person's power—and survive. I must be comfortable with my own power to such a degree that I can trust myself to handle my rage, to moderate my self-interest.

These mature resources are essential in "fighting fair" in intimate relationships; they are also necessary for effective collaboration in work. These strengths enable me to work out differences with colleagues, to mediate disputes, and to work through conflict. These resources are also important in my struggle to function with integrity as a member of the "loyal opposition."

With these resources of mature contesting, I know that I am strong enough to risk the fight, trusting that I will survive—whether I win or lose. This conviction gives me courage to enter the social arena with other powerful adults.

Power For

Another way in which I come to a sense of personal power is in an awareness that "I am strong for others." Many responsibilities of adulthood call out this special kind of strength. As a coworker, I give my talent to the tasks of the team. As a parent, I marshal my resources to care for my children. As a designated leader, I use my influence to further the goals of the group. My ability to have an impact and to make a difference is focused outside myself. I spend myself and my resources in pursuit of someone else's benefit.

At its best, this impulse is expressed in nurturance. I am powerful enough to participate in creating something new—our child or a joint project or a shared dream. Beyond this movement of creativity, I can use my power in care, in support of this new life on its own terms. The crucial phrase here, of course, is "on its own terms." The challenge of nurturance is to be able to use my power for others in ways that empower rather than diminish them, in ways that increase their freedom rather than make them more dependent on me.

We sense how tricky this can be for the parent, to care for growing children not by forcing them to become "my best idea" of who they should be but by fostering their growth into the persons they are in their own right. The task is no less tricky for the leader or the counselor or the person in ministry. Our responsibilities require us to use our power for other adults. We come in touch with the ambiguity involved in the use of our power "for their sake." This is the tension between care and constraint.

When I know myself to be strong in regard to another's need, a feeling of dominance may be provoked. Power and need are not shared between us. One of us may emerge as "strong" in the relationship and the other as "weak." This perception of a power imbalance can be destructive in a relationship between adults.

Mature relationships between adults are characterized by mutuality, even where strict "equality" is neither necessary nor possible. We cannot be exactly equal in intelligence, physical strength, social graces, and other abilities. The challenge of mutuality invites us to become engaged with one another's strengths and weaknesses. You can see and embrace both my strengths and my limits; I can acknowledge and support both your gifts and your weaknesses. Such mutuality neither demands nor pretends to be a total equality. By recognizing and even celebrating differences of strength, we protect ourselves from the genuine imbalances of paternalism and dependency. Without an active commitment to mutuality, I can gradually slip into identifying your good with my sense of "what is good for you." An attitude that begins in altruistic care can shift toward condescension. The illusion here is to judge that I know better than you what is in your best interests; it is a temptation to which many in ministry and other helping professions may be especially prone.

But "power for" remains an important resource of adult maturity. When the arrogance of "I know better than you what is in your best interests" can be recognized, the strengths of generative care can be released. These are essential for the responsibilities of parenting; they are crucial in religious leadership as well.

Power With

The fifth face of adult power is "power with." This experience is rooted in the conviction that "we are strong together." In our coming together, I know myself to be strong. Your strength does not diminish me or replace my own. Instead it increases and enhances my strength. My power is in part a strength that is shared. The experience here is that of interdependence—the ability to enjoy *mutual* influence and *mutual* empowerment. This resource draws on the matured strengths of dependability—a "dependability" that goes both ways.

For the benefits of interdependence to be available to me I must, first, *be able to depend on others*. I need the conviction, born in part of experience and in part of trust, that I do not have to do it by myself. This capacity for dependence is not the kind of *dependency* so feared by most Americans: the inability to care for my own needs that leaves me at the mercy of others. It is not the dependency that therapists see in the person who characteristically uses his needs to manipulate those around him. Rather it is a strength of dependence: I am strong enough to receive and benefit from others' power. It is because I know myself to be (somewhat) strong that I can allow my weaknesses to be visible to myself and to others as well. My weaknesses are not stronger than my strengths. So I need not consume my energies in the endless and futile effort to hide my limitations; I need not spend my strength in self-defense.

Such mature dependence is grounded in *having received* strength and nurturance from the "outside," from other people in my environment. Having received this strength from beyond myself, I become strong enough now to meet my own needs and those of other people as well.

In work this enables me to trust your talent to supplement my own. I know that your abilities can compensate in areas where I am not strong. I can admit my limits and rejoice in the resources that you bring to our common tasks.

In the close relationships of friendship and marriage, I come to trust that your strength will be there for me when I need it. I learn that it is safe to share my vulnerability and to acknowledge how much I need you. I need not fear that this will lessen me in your eyes or that you will turn away in disgust. The adult strength of mutuality grows out of this shared ability to depend.

Interdependence requires that I be able to depend on others; it also demands that I be able *to let others depend on me*. This means that I can make my strength available in ways that empower others rather than diminish them. I am not intimidated by other people's strength, nor am I frightened by their weakness. I can be counted on by other people. I know how to let them lean on me without seducing them to become lasting dependents. I can care beyond control.

This sense of "power with," then, may be experienced in both love and collaboration. We count on one another to bring different resources to our common task. We rely on one another's strengths to make up for the limits we each have. And beyond this, we are aware that when we come together there is power available that goes beyond what was originally ours. In *Insight and Responsibility*, Erik Erikson speaks of this experience of "power with." "In relationships of full mutuality, the sharing goes beyond self-disclosure toward interpenetration of lives...[as] partners depend on each other for the development of their respective strengths." In this family or diocese or congregation, our communal effort is richer because our powers have come together. The fruit of "power with" goes beyond the achievement of goals to include the enrichment of each of us and of our shared life.

Power and Weakness

Any serious discussion of maturity must confront both power and weakness. Adult life does not simply lead us out of impotence into strength. That is a fantasy of adolescence. Maturity asks, instead, a befriending of ourselves as both weak and strong. Its challenge is not to determine whether I am strong or weak. To that question the only honest answer can be "Yes." We are, each of us, a blend of characteristic strengths and enduring weaknesses.

In chapter six we explored the dual movement of conversion calling us to turn away from our sinfulness even as we become more tolerant of the weakness that remains. This image of strength in weakness is not unfamiliar to the Christian.

The gospels tell a story of strength and failure: Jesus' power to call us to pursue the kingdom was not lessened by his inability to protect himself from death. "He was crucified in weakness, but lives by the power of God" (2 Corinthians 13:4).

Saint Paul's letters explore and celebrate, with a special enthusiasm, the paradox of power and weakness in Christian life. At the end of his second letter to the Christians in Corinth, Paul reveals a personal difficulty: this strong, assertive minister was afflicted by "a thorn in the flesh." Troubled and humiliated by this weakness, he prayed to God to remove it from his life. But it did not disappear. In its enduring presence in his life, Paul sensed God's response: "power is made perfect in weakness" (2 Corinthians 12:9). Not "my power will overcome your weakness" or "my power is unconcerned with weakness," but "my power is at its best in weakness." This peculiar attitude toward personal weakness led Paul to say to those in Corinth, "I am content with weaknesses...for whenever I am weak, then I am strong" (12:10). If we are not quite content with our weaknesses, we can at least confirm, from our experience, that God seems to enjoy working through them. Often we accomplish things due to our abilities, and we give thanks. And not infrequently our abilities fail us; we are not strong enough to meet some challenge or problem. And yet, despite our failure, the problem or challenge is met. Nor is it that God skirts our weakness. Often enough, God's graceful results seem to arrive directly through our weakness.

We learn very gradually the Christian paradox of power. We are invited to grow strong and become virtuous, and we are called to befriend those enduring weaknesses that God sees fit to leave with us and through which God delights to act.

This paradox can help us heal some of the distress around power and leadership in the Church. The leaders in the community of faith are not meant to be powerful, self-sufficient, without need. They are, in an ancient image, wounded healers. Ministry and healing are often provided by the weak in order, as we remember, to confound the strong. Leaders—and this makes them one with us and rescues them from a splendid isolation as "superiors"—are both strong and weak. Like any adult they are gifted and flawed. This humanness of Church leaders should remind us not to project idealized, impossible expectations on them. This humanness also invites us to re-imagine leadership as a service within the community. Such a leadership, not isolated in its own power (and forced to conceal its weakness), will be able to take better advantage of the power and gifts available in the community. And the inequality of strengths in the group will not be a scandal but an invitation to mutuality—a sharing of power and weakness.

Reflective Exercise

Consider the experience of personal power in your own life by returning to the chart that appears on page 98.

1. Recall instances of your own power in each of these five different faces. Be as concrete as you can; go to particular events and situations of the past year or so. Spend time with these memories and the feelings that accompany them.
2. Which of these faces of personal power is most character-istic of you? Why do you think this is the case?
3. Which is least characteristic of you? Why is this so?
4. What change, if any, would you like to see in the balance among these expressions of power in your life these days?

Then take time to savor the paradox of "power through weakness" in your own life. First, recall a recent situation in which you were aware of God working through your weak-ness. Bring to mind again the people and circumstances and out-come. Then spend several moments in prayer, giving thanks for this special way in which the power of God moves through you.

About the Authors

Evelyn Eaton Whitehead is a developmental psychologist who holds a Ph.D. from the University of Chicago. James D. Whitehead, pastoral theologian and historian of religion, received a Ph.D. from Harvard University. The Whiteheads have been affiliated with the Institute of Pastoral Studies at Loyola University Chicago since 1970, which is also the year of their marriage.

Since 1998 the Whiteheads have traveled annually to China to offer university courses and lectures in Shanghai, Nanjing, Hangzhou, and in Hong Kong. Currently they are Distinguished Fellows of the EDS-Steward Chair in the Ricci Institute for Chinese-Western Cultural History at the University of San Francisco.